ACTS *of* HARLOTRY

ACTS *of* HARLOTRY

Within the Body of Christ

ALISHA N. SCOTT

Nabi House Publishing

ACTS OF HARLOTRY WITHIN THE BODY OF CHRIST
By Alisha N. Scott
Published by Nabi House Publishing
www.AlishaNScott.com
Alisha@alishanscott.com

Unless otherwise noted, all Scripture quotations are from the Amplified Bible. Old Testament copyright © 1965, 1987 by the Zondervan Cooperation. The Amplified New Testament copyright © 1954, 1958, 1987 by the Zondervan Cooperation. Used by permission.

Scripture quotations marked KJV are from the King James Version of the Bible.

Scripture quotations marked NIV are from the Holy Bible, New International Version. Copyright © 1973, 1978, 1987 by the Lockman Foundation. Used by permission.

Scripture quotations marked NKJV are from the New King James Version of the Bible. Copyright © 1979, 1980, 1982 by Thomas Nelson., Inc. Used by permission.

ISBN-13: 978-0615676289

ISBN-10: 0615676286

First Edition

14 13 12 11 10 / 10 9 8 7 6 5 4 3 2 1

Printed in the United States of America

DEDICATION

TO MY GOD and Best Friend, You make my heart smile. To my parents, Roosevelt and Bernice Scott, for always showing undying support and love. To my grandparents, Garfield and Mattie Freeman & Roosevelt and Maebell Scott Sr. for loving God. To Xavier, Cameron, Kynnadi, Kayla, Kaleb, and Morgan for bringing a smile to my face no matter what :)

ACKNOWLEDGEMENTS

FIRST AND FOREMOST , I would like give thanks to my God, the one and only true and living God. He alone has given me the strength and the motivation to finish the task at hand. I thank my sisters Robin Scott-Moore, Cassandra Scott-Jean, and Kimberly Scott- Sumbry for always being there no matter what. To my aunts Patricia Crawford, Ann Thomas, Jean Webb, Leona Laster, Mattie Shiloh and Shirley Cook, thank you for being so wonderful. Thank you, Pastor Eddie and Sonya Adams of Victory Tabernacle for your love and encouragement. Javaz Williams, thank you for allowing me to share a very special dream given to you by God in Chapter 5. To a great editor, Jevon Bolden, thank you for the time you spent editing this book. Thank you, Beatrice Wooden for your positive outlook and for proofreading my manuscript, wonderful job. Pastor Mary Helen Williams and Torida Graham-Easley, thank you for your kindness and remarkable wisdom. Angela Jackson-Figgins and Vonda Stubbs, thank you for being supportive of this assignment. Thank you to a very special team of friends, colleagues, and fellow church members who have in some way encouraged me during this undertaking: Donna Gardner, Emily Addison, Rev. Marvin and Darlene Taylor, Jamillah Smith, Patrisha Stills, Barbara Martin, Sakim Burns, Helen Usher, Wendy Nix, Ladonna Barge, Vernester Williams, Sheena Cash, Michelle Smith, Janice Newberry, Angela Hicks-Barnes, and Catherine Greene.

CONTENTS

PREFACE

When Israel was a child, then I loved him and
called My son out of Egypt. The more [the
prophets] called to them, the more they went
from them; they kept sacrificing to the Baals
and burning incense to the graven images. Yet
I taught Ephraim to walk, taking them by
their arms or taking them up in My arms, but
they did not know that I healed them. I drew
them with cords of a man, with bands of love,
and I was to them as one who lifts up and
eases the yoke over their cheeks, and I bent
down to them and gently laid food before
them. They shall not [literally] return into
[another bondage in] the land of Egypt, but
the Assyrian shall be their king because they
refused to return to Me. And the sword shall
rage against and fall upon their cities and shall
consume the bars of their gates and shall
make an end [of their defenses], because of
their own counsels and devices. My people are
bent on backsliding from Me; though [the
prophets] call them to Him Who is on high,
none at all will exalt Him or lift himself up [to
come to Him].

—HOSEA 11:1–7

IN AN ERA of degradation, debauchery, and
idolatry—despite many warnings from God—the
children of Israel continued to engage in all
manner of lewdness before His face. Forsaking
the sanctity of the covenant made with Him, they
foolishly pursued worthless idols in His stead. Instead

11

of turning their hearts in repentance, they turned a deaf ear to the counsel of the Lord.

> Therefore have I hewn down and smitten them by means of the prophets; I have slain them by the words of My mouth; My judgments [pronounced upon them by you prophets] are like the light that goes forth.
>
> —Hosea 6:5

Because God is merciful and abundant in grace, in response to their hardened hearts, He raised up prophets with faces set like flint. God commissioned them with hard words that were sharp enough to pierce darkened hearts with light and truth in hopes that His people would turn to Him in repentance. "When He slew [some of] them, [the remainder] inquired after Him diligently, and they repented and sincerely sought God [for a time]" (Psalm 78:34).

Today we live in an era of apostasy much like that of the children of Israel and as spiritual darkness attempts to blanket the earth, the people of God must arise and present the light of the gospel of Christ uncompromisingly and unadulterated. Collectively and unashamed, we must proclaim the true Message of Christ, because it is only by the truth that lives are saved, delivered, and set free. It is only by proclaiming the truth, that darkness is exposed. Hebrews 4:12 says:

> For the Word that God speaks is alive and full of power [making it active, operative, energizing, and effective]; it is sharper than any two edged sword, penetrating to the dividing line of the breath of life (soul) and [the immortal] spirit, and of joints and marrow [of the deepest parts of our nature],

exposing and sifting and analyzing and judging the very thoughts and purposes of the heart.

On writing *Acts of Harlotry*, my assignment is to shed light within the body of Christ by speaking the truth in love. Nearly four years ago, this assignment was awakened in my spirit by a dream from the Lord. In this dream, I saw a valley of mountains. Upon one of the monstrous mountains stood several leaders dressed in priestly garments. Below the mountain was a man who desperately searched for Jesus. Unable to find Him, the frantic man eventually climbed the mountain where the leaders stood proudly. "Where is Jesus?" he asked, out of breath from the arduous hike. Pointing down the mountain, the priestly leaders looked at him with hatred in their eyes and replied, "He's down there, and it's your fault!" Disappointed, the man gazed back down the mountain where he had once been and saw Jesus walking calmly but intensely over the earth. He was searching as well. "For the eyes of the Lord run to and fro throughout the whole earth to show Himself strong in behalf of those whose hearts are blameless toward Him"(2 Chr. 16:9).

After I awoke from the dream, the Lord spoke clearly to me saying, "My people are searching for Me and I am searching for them. False doctrine separates Me from My children. Truly, they don't know who I Am. There are people in high places leading My flock astray and these false leaders will be brought down from their self-proclaimed platforms. It is time for those I have truly called to replace them. Lead My sheep to the One who seeks harder after them than they do Me. I love them so much." (*December 13, 2008*)

In this hour, the eyes of the Lord are running throughout the earth searching for hearts that are truly devoted to and desperate for Him. He's searching for those who hunger and thirst after righteousness. (See Matthew 5:6.) In the dream, the leaders were enraged because Jesus was not upon the mountain tops where they stood grandiosely. Because they had become high and lifted up in pride, Jesus was walking in the valley searching for the meek and humble servants. God is now elevating His true leaders to bring down the spirits of harlotry running rampant across the nation and within the body of Christ.

There will be a clear distinction between those truly called of the Lord and those who are not. One distinction is that this remnant won't profess a "new gospel." Upon their lips will be the truth combined with fervor, faith, and power in a greater measure than that of the prophets of old. They will not promote the popular gospel of demons or "fleshy" feel-good messages. Proclaiming the true gospel of Christ, this remnant will boast of the Lord promoting holiness, consecration, and righteousness. They won't come in with "words of eloquence" but in demonstration of power. Crying out and sparing not against wickedness, these true end-time ministers will be equipped with the ability to call fire down from heaven, setting ablaze the things that are not of God.

Within the pages of this book, we will examine Israel's harlotry in comparison to modern-day spiritual harlotry in the body of Christ. The purpose of this book is to prepare the body of Christ for the shift that is to take place regarding those who have been entrusted with preaching the Word of God, yet have been guilty of facilitating lies and tainting it for selfishness and greed. Those seated upon well-known platforms that have been found untrustworthy of being messengers of the gospel will be dethroned because of their own waywardness and deceit. (See 1 Thessalonians 2:3–5.) We will also take an in-depth look at the principalities, powers, and rulers of darkness responsible for facilitating spiritual harlotry within the body. Furthermore, we will discuss the dethroning of said demonic forces.

This book is full of truth and light that will shine upon the darkness of deception that has been implanted into the hearts of the multitudes. It is a "killing" word with the intention to seek and destroy spiritual falsehood. It is an attempt to murder everything moving in this hour that is not of God.

> Cry aloud, spare not. Lift up your voice like a trumpet and declare to My people their transgression and to the house of Jacob their sins! Yet they seek, inquire for, and require Me daily and delight [externally] to know My ways, as [if they were in reality] a nation that did righteousness and forsook not the ordinance of their God. They ask of Me righteous judgments, they delight to draw near to God [in visible ways].
>
> —ISAIAH 58:1–2

INTRODUCTION

Let marriage be held in honor (esteemed
worthy, precious, of great price, and especially
dear) in all things. And thus let the marriage
bed be undefiled (kept undishonored); for
God will judge and punish the unchaste [all
guilty of sexual vice] and adulterous.

—HEBREWS 13:4

GOD MAKES IT evident from the very
beginning that He esteems the institution of
marriage highly. Marriage is precious in His
sight because it expresses His heart towards
humanity. It mimics the relationship He desires to
share with us as His children. While marriage
expresses the highest level of intimacy shared
between man and wife, the intimacy shared between
man and God is higher. Genesis 2:22–24 tells of the
first marital union:

> And the rib or part of his side which the Lord
> God had taken from the man He built up and
> made into a woman, and He brought her to
> the man. Then Adam said, This [creature] is
> now bone of my bones and flesh of my flesh;
> she shall be called Woman, because she was
> taken out of a man. Therefore a man shall
> leave his father and his mother and shall
> become united and cleave to his wife, and
> they shall become one flesh.

When two are joined together in marriage, they
are spiritually united and because marriage is a

17

spiritual union, it is not to be taken lightly. Marriage defies mathematical logic in that one plus one no longer equals two; it equals one. Two becomes one flesh, one mind, and one heart. This is why as Christians we are instructed not to be unequally yoked together with unbelievers. In doing so, we risk the possibility of becoming united to someone whose heart does not belong to the Lord. (See 2 Corinthians 6:14.) An unequally yoked union is dangerous because when the shared heart is not yielded to God, there is room for the division of affections. If the heart of the union is divided, then adultery has the opportunity to sneak in.

The children of Israel were all too familiar with divided hearts, so much so, that God said "I will give them one heart [a new heart] and I will put a new spirit within them; and I will take the stony [unnaturally hardened] heart out of their flesh, and will give them a heart of flesh [sensitive and responsive to the touch of their God], that they may walk in My statutes and keep My ordinances, and do them. And they shall be My people, and I will be their God"(Ezek.11:19–20).The New International Version says, "I will give them an undivided heart." Israel's affections had become so divided that there was no longer space in their adulterous hearts for their Groom.

The word *adultery* comes from the Hebrew word *na'aph*[1] which means "to apostatize." To *apostatize*[2] is "to forsake or abandon one's belief, faith, or allegiance." Therefore, spiritual adultery or harlotry not only involves committing sexual sin or describes an individual who steps outside of the boundaries of marriage, but it also describes one who forsakes his faith seeking after another. It is one who forsakes the true and living God for an idol. So, while physical adultery involves turning the heart from the spouse and toward another person, spiritual harlotry involves turning the heart from God and toward wickedness.

Harlotry begins in the heart; the body follows the directions of the heart, which leads to acts of harlotry. "Whoever looks at a woman lustfully, he has already committed adultery with her in his heart" (Matt. 5:28). The act of sex outside of marriage is only one of many manifestations of the spiritual abandonment that has already taken place inside of an estranged heart.

Within the body of Christ, hearts are becoming alienated and being seduced into the arms of deception. Hearts are persistently being turned toward unrighteousness and idolatry by way of false doctrine. As a result, we have begun to divorce the Lord in the spirit. Malachi 2:14–16 says:

> Yet you ask, Why does He reject it? Because the Lord was witness [to the covenant made at your marriage] between you and the wife of your youth, against whom you have dealt treacherously and to whom you were faithless. Yet she is your companion and the wife of your covenant [made by your marriage vows]. And did not God make [you and your wife] one [flesh]? Did not One make you and preserve your spirit alive? And why [did God make you two] one? Because He sought a godly offspring [from your union]. Therefore take heed to yourselves, and let no one deal treacherously and be faithless to the wife of his youth. For the Lord, the God of Israel, says: I hate divorce and marital separation and him who covers his garment [his wife] with violence. Therefore keep a watch upon your

19

spirit [that it may be controlled by My Spirit],
that you deal not treacherously and faithlessly
[with your marriage mate].

God considers marriage a covenant—a binding
promise—and He considers divorce violent because it
fights against His plan and attacks His purpose for
marriage. The Book of Deuteronomy expounds upon
the marriage contract between God and His bride,
Israel. Obedience to the covenant promised the
blessings of God while disobedience promised a
curse. Jeremiah 3:1, 14 says:

> That is to say, If a man puts away his wife and
> she goes from him and becomes another
> man's, will he return to her again? [Of course
> not!] Would not that land [where such a thing
> happened] be greatly polluted? But you have
> played the harlot [against Me] with many
> lovers—yet would you now return to Me?
> says the Lord [or do you even think to return
> to Me?]....Return, O faithless children [of the
> whole twelve tribes], says the Lord, for I am
> Lord *and* Master *and* Husband to you, and I
> will take you [not as a nation, but
> individually]—one from a city and two from a
> tribal family—and I will bring you to Zion.

Israel was God's chosen bride, yet she rejected
Him through her disobedience. She was brazen,
allowing herself to be polluted by her infidelities. She
continued to do what was evil in the sight of the Lord
despite counsel and correction. First Samuel 8:5–8
says:

> And said to him, Behold, you are old, and
> your sons do not walk in your ways; now
> appoint us a king to rule over us like all the
> other nations. But it displeased Samuel when
> they said, Give us a king to govern us. And
> Samuel prayed to the Lord. And the Lord said

> to Samuel, Hearken to the voice of the people
> in all they say to you; for they have not
> rejected you, but they have rejected Me, that I
> should not be King over them. According to
> all the works which they have done since I
> brought them up out of Egypt even to this
> day, forsaking Me and serving other gods, so
> they also do to you.

Israel no longer wanted God as her Husband, King, or Source. Instead, she desired to be led by man. She traded in her gown of brilliant white to wear the rags of harlotry upon her back. She chose to be the whore of the world, rather than the bride of God.

I dreamed of two brothers who both had been caught in the act of adultery by their spouses. What intrigued me the most about this dream was their nonchalant attitude toward being caught; they laughed about their infidelity as if it was no great offense. In fact, even though the younger brother stepped outside of his marital vows, he was adamant that what he had done was not morally wrong or *technically* considered adultery. Worn around his neck was a silver necklace with a tree engraved on it. Underneath the tree was the word *blessed*. After remembering the necklace was around his neck, he immediately showed it to his older brother. However, it was interesting that only after committing adultery did he decide to look around his neck remembering that he was attempting to curse what God had blessed, the institution of marriage. How easy it is to forget the commandments of God when they are only worn topically and not bound upon our hearts. Proverbs 6:20–26 says:

> My son, keep your father's [God-given]
> commandment and forsake not the law of

21

[God] your mother [taught you]. Bind them continually upon your heart and tie them about your neck. When you go, they [the words of your parents' God] shall lead you; when you sleep, they shall keep you; and when you waken, they shall talk with you. For the commandment is a lamp, and the whole teaching [of the law] is light, and reproofs of discipline are the way of life, to keep you from the evil woman, from the flattery of the tongue of a loose woman. Lust not after her beauty in your heart, neither let her capture you with her eyelids. For on account of a harlot a man is brought to a piece of bread, and the adulteress stalks and snares [as with a hook] the precious life [of a man].

If the Word of God was truly bound upon our hearts night and day, then we could not continuously fall for the seductive schemes of the enemy. If the commandments of the Lord were hidden inside of our hearts, harlotry would have no place to dwell and we would not sin against Him. (See Psalm 119:11.) Spiritual harlotry amongst those who profess Christ is prevalent because the commandments of God have become afterthoughts and many have chosen to wear the necklace of pride instead. (See Psalm 73:6.) Jeremiah 3:2-3, 7-8 reads:

Lift up your eyes to the bare heights and see. Where have you not been adulterously lain with? By the wayside you have sat waiting for lovers [eager for idolatry], like an Arabian [desert tribesman who waits to plunder] in the wilderness; and you have polluted the land with your vile harlotry and your wickedness (unfaithfulness and disobedience to God). Therefore the showers have been withheld, and there has been no spring rain. Yet you have the brow of a prostitute; you refuse to be

> ashamed.... And I said, After she has done all
> these things, she will return to Me; but she did
> not return, and her faithless and treacherous
> sister Judah saw it. And I saw, even though
> [Judah knew] that for this very cause of
> committing adultery (idolatry) I [the Lord] had
> put faithless Israel away and given her a bill of
> divorce; yet her faithless and treacherous
> sister Judah was not afraid, but she also went
> and played the harlot [following after idols].

Playing the harlot against God, the children of
Israel further polluted themselves through persistent
acts of unfaithfulness. Weary from their harlotry, God
finally issued them a certificate of divorce.

For Christians, marriage is a beautiful depiction of
the relationship between Christ and His bride, the
church. However, the pollution of the world is
influencing the body of Christ in unprecedented ways.
We are commanded in 1 John 2:15 "Do not love or
cherish the world or the things that are in the world."
There should be a noticeable distinction between the
world and the church; however, lines are crossed
more often than not. Galatians 2:11–14 reads:

> But when Cephas (Peter) came to Antioch, I
> protested and opposed him to his face
> [concerning his conduct there], for he was
> blameable and stood condemned. For up to
> the time that certain persons came from
> James, he ate his meals with the Gentile
> [converts]; but when the men [from
> Jerusalem] arrived, he withdrew and held
> himself aloof from the Gentiles and [ate]
> separately for fear of those of the
> circumcision [party]. And the rest of the Jews
> along with him also concealed their true
> convictions and acted insincerely, with the
> result that even Barnabas was carried away by
> their hypocrisy (their example of insincerity

and pretense). But as soon as I saw that they were not straightforward *and* were not living up to the truth of the Gospel, I said to Cephas (Peter) before everybody present, If you, though born a Jew, can live [as you have been living] like a Gentile and not like a Jew, how do you dare now to urge *and* practically force the Gentiles to [comply with the ritual of Judaism and] live like Jews?

Like Peter, many are putting on false pretenses with one foot in the world and the other in the pulpit. However, we must have hearts truly devoted to God at all times and not only when it is convenient. We must not be ashamed of the full gospel of Jesus Christ.

> But now I write to you not to associate with anyone who bears the name of [Christian] brother if he is known to be guilty of immorality or greed, or is an idolater [whose soul is devoted to any object that usurps the place of God], or is a person with a foul tongue [railing, abusing, reviling, slandering], or is a drunkard or a swindler or a robber. [No] you must not so much as eat with such a person.
>
> —1 CORINTHIANS 5:11

2 Kings 4:3 8-41 says:

> Elisha came back to Gilgal during a famine in the land. The sons of the prophets were sitting before him, and he said to his servant, Set on the big pot and cook pottage for the sons of the prophets. Then one went into the field to gather herbs and gathered from a wild vine his lap full of wild gourds, and returned and cut them up into the pot of pottage, for they were unknown to them. So they poured

24

> it out for the men to eat. But as they ate of the
> pottage, they cried out, O man of God, there
> is death in the pot! And they could not eat it.
> But he said, Bring meal [as a symbol of God's
> healing power]. And he cast it into the pot
> and said, Pour it out for the people that they
> may eat. Then there was no harm in the pot.

There was a famine in Gilgal and the children of God were hungry and thus scavenging for food to eat. Unknowingly, one of Elisha's sons sliced harmful, wild ingredients into the stew making it "death in a pot." It was lethal. The pot of stew is symbolic of the way spiritual food is being handled for the people of God in this hour. There are many spiritually immature, self imposed leaders in the body of Christ who have become misguided. They have begun to add lethal, hazardous lies to God's perfect recipe which causes His children to die spiritual deaths. After the sons of Elisha realized that they were in error, they turned to the voice of God for help.

Because there is famine in the land, false prophets are emerging in God's name, feeding His people their own recipe which leads to spiritual suicide. Thus, we must be ever so mindful of where we are being fed, because as the ways of the world penetrate the very walls of the house of God, many of those entrusted with proclaiming the Word are making deadly alliances and forsaking all that they have known as truth. Second Peter 2:13–14 reads:

> Being destined to receive [punishment as] the
> reward of [their] unrighteousness [suffering
> wrong as the hire for their wrongdoing]. They
> count it a delight to revel in the daytime
> [living luxuriously and delicately]. They are
> blots and blemishes, reveling in their
> deceptions and carousing together [even] as

> they feast with you. They have eyes full of
> harlotry, insatiable for sin. They beguile and
> bait and lure away unstable souls. Their hearts
> are trained in covetousness (lust, greed), [they
> are] children of a curse [exposed to cursing]!

Doctrines of demons and warped versions of Scripture are now promoted to accommodate individual lusts and cravings. Christianity is now remolded and reshaped into what suits a particular audience. Holiness and righteousness are topics that have become antiquated and are increasingly replaced with self-help topics and sugar-coated messages of prosperity without righteousness. The truth is more than often withheld.

> I am surprised and astonished that you are so
> quickly turning renegade and deserting Him
> Who invited and called you by the grace
> (unmerited favor) of Christ (the Messiah) [and
> that you are transferring your allegiance] to a
> different [even an opposition] gospel. Not
> that there is [or could be] any other [genuine
> Gospel], but there are [obviously] some who
> are troubling and disturbing and bewildering
> you with a different kind of teaching which
> they offer as a gospel] and want to pervert and
> distort the Gospel of Christ (the Messiah)
> [into something which it absolutely is not].
>
> —GALATIANS 1:6–7

Those preaching sermons of this caliber gain notoriety and fame because they do not confront the darkness of sin. However, God is shining light upon the false, empty, and fruitless vision and flattering divination in His house. (See Ezekiel 12:24.) The Word of God must not be altered. It is imperative that we cease putting more effort into "pulpit performances" than we do with speaking the truth.

Inventory must be taken to discover whom it is we are attempting to please, men or God (Gal. 1:10). Doom is inevitable for those who seek to please man by compromising the Word of God. As degradation escalates and false prophets emerge, I can only make a statement that many may find redundant: we are living in the last days and the church must begin to prepare herself for the Bridegroom. Ephesians 5:23–27 says:

> For the husband is head of the wife as Christ is the Head of the church, Himself the Savior of [His] body. As the church is subject to Christ, so let wives also be subject in everything to their husbands. Husbands, love your wives, as Christ loved the church and gave Himself up for her, So that He might sanctify her, having cleansed her by the washing of water with the Word, that He might present the church to Himself in glorious splendor, without spot or wrinkle or any such things [that she might be holy and faultless].

The spots of iniquity must be vanquished, but this will only happen as we, God's people, arise in truth. Spiritual darkness is gaining momentum in these final days with an attempt to cover the earth as a mantle. Though Satan's demise is inevitable, we as the body of Christ must dethrone the principalities, powers, and rulers of spiritual wickedness responsible for the spread of spiritual harlotry. God has given us the enemy's neck. The battle is won, but the fight rages. Thus we must pick up our weapon, the inerrant word of God, and engage.

1

THE ART *of* THE APOTHECARY

> Mary took a pound of ointment of pure liquid
> nard [a rare perfume] that was very expensive,
> and she poured it on Jesus' feet and wiped
> them with her hair. And the whole house was
> filled with the fragrance of the perfume.
>
> —JOHN 12:3

AS A LOVER of fine fragrances, I've learned that the more costly a perfume, oftentimes the more pleasing its aroma. However, I have also found that the expensiveness of designer fragrances has opened up the door for the marketing of cheap imposter or counterfeit fragrances. Purchasing a bottle of the counterfeit perfume is tempting, because it often looks like the original, is packaged like the original, and for a moment smells remarkably like the original. However, while imposters have the ability to mimic the smell of designer fragrances, it is often short-lived and moments later, the scent is gone, it reeks of a strange odor, or some other adverse reaction occurs. Why? It's because the formulators of counterfeit fragrances are more concerned with the presentation of the product than they are with the ingredients used to formulate it.

In fact, it has been found that counterfeiters use contaminated alcohol, antifreeze, urine, and other harmful bacteria in compounding their fragrances. They have also been found guilty of mixing a few ingredients of quality with the putrid ingredients mentioned above. The strange mixture is hazardous because the disgusting ingredients used could lead to blindness, coma, allergic reactions, and even death.

In a dream, I watched the mother of a nationally known and proven prophet of the Lord discuss how her daughter was barely recognizable after a severe allergic reaction occurred which deformed and then killed her. Many within the body of Christ have been spiritually blinded and placed into spiritual comas because of the falsehood being sprayed upon them from pulpits across the nation. The Enemy is attempting to kill the truth, overpowering it with the stench of false doctrine mixed with some truth. This is the same age-old tactic of Satan that originated in the Garden of Eden. This foul mixture of truth and lies causes a severe allergic reaction resulting in spiritual death. We see a similar strange mixture described in Hosea 7:8 which says:

> Ephraim mixes himself among the peoples [courting the favor of first one country, then another]; Ephraim is a cake not turned.

Isaiah 1:21–22 also reads:

> How the faithful city has become an [idolatrous] harlot, she who was full of justice! Uprightness and right standing with God [once] lodged in her—but now murderers. Your silver has become dross, your wine is mixed with water.

The word *mixed* as it is used above implies that God's children had become "impure and adulterated or mixed with impurities." The bride of God, Israel, became harlotrous, intertwined with the habits and customs of their idolatrous neighboring countries. They were guilty of creating an unholy concoction, which resulted in a foreign strange smell that not only put a bad taste in the mouth of God, but came up as a stench into His nostrils. Isaiah 57:8–10 says:

> Behind the door and the doorpost you have set up your [idol] symbol [as a substitute for the Scripture text God ordered]. Deserting Me, you have uncovered and ascended and enlarged your bed; and you have made a [fresh] bargain for yourself with [the adulterers], and you loved their bed, where you saw [a beckoning hand or a passion-inflaming image].And you went to the king [of foreign lands with gifts] or to Molech [the god] with oil and increased your perfumes and ointments; you sent your messengers far off and debased yourself even to Sheol (Hades) [symbol of an abysmal depth of degradation]. You were wearied with the length of your way [in trying to find rest and satisfaction in alliances apart from the true God], yet you did not say, There is no result or profit. You found quickened strength; therefore you were not faint or heartsick [or penitent].

Reaching into the depths of degradation, Israel began to create her own symbols and words, substituting them for God's. She covenanted with false gods, forsaking the fragrance of the true and living God for the counterfeit scent of a harlot. Hosea 12:1 says:

> Ephraim herds and feeds on the wind and
> pursues the [parching] east wind; every day he
> increases lies and violence, and a covenant is
> made with Assyria and oil is carried to Egypt.

The children of Israel sought after the fleeting, temporal pleasures of the flesh. They carried precious oil away to Egypt to seek their favor and assistance. Sadly, many professing Christians have become guilty of this very offense. They have begun to substitute the truth of God with their own fables and the anointing is now being prostituted for wealth, notoriety, and prosperity. It is often misused, abused, and carried into the world for selfish purposes. Second Corinthians 2:14–17 says:

> But thanks be to God, Who in Christ always
> leads us in triumph [as trophies of Christ's
> victory] and through us spreads and makes
> evident the fragrance of the knowledge of
> God everywhere, For we are the sweet
> fragrance of Christ [which exhales] unto God,
> [discernible alike] among those who are being
> saved and among those who are perishing: To
> the latter it is an aroma [wafted] from death to
> death [a fatal odor, the smell of doom]; to the
> former it is an aroma from life to life [a vital
> fragrance, living and fresh]. And who is
> qualified (fit and sufficient) for these things?
> [Who is able for such a ministry? We?] For we
> are not, like so many, [like hucksters making a
> trade of] peddling God's Word [shortchanging
> and adulterating the divine message]; but like
> [men] of sincerity and the purest motive, as
> [commissioned and sent] by God, we speak
> [His message] in Christ (the Messiah), in the
> [very] sight and presence of God.

The dying world, those living carnally have a repulsive odor; the smell of death is upon them. As

Christians, we are to spread the knowledge of Christ, which is as a sweet fragrance to a world that is dead in religion and rotten with immorality. We are to be a pleasant aroma to a world that is hurting, hungry, thirsty, poor, and broken. And instead of perverting the gospel to gain notoriety from the world, we should promote the gospel to gain the perverse for the Kingdom.

In verse 17, the word *adulterate* means to "cheapen the Word of God for profit." When water is added to even the most fragrant perfume, it is cheapened and the consistency changes. It is therefore no longer qualified to be called that particular fragrance. From the point that water is added, it is considered a weakened imposter.

Many have forsaken the fragrance of Christ because of its expense. Cheapening Christianity makes it affordable to all. Many have proceeded to concoct strange versions of the original. The gospel of Christ is cheapened by individuals who water it down, and because water has been added it is no longer considered the gospel of Christ, but a counterfeit. And they, as leaders, are no longer considered ministers of the gospel, but harlotrous imposters. It is now popular to be considered a Christian because imposters have lowered the cost.

> From the sole of the foot even to the head there is no soundness or health in [the nation's body]—but wounds and bruises and fresh and bleeding stripes; they have not been pressed out and closed up or bound up or softened with oil. [No one has troubled to seek a remedy.]
>
> —ISAIAH 1:6

The body of Christ is seriously ill with sin. Why? False leaders are peddling the Word of God within the body of Christ as common, brazen harlots peddle their bodies in the world. They are responsible for putrefying the gospel for the sake of complacency. Proclaiming flesh driven messages, the very name of Jesus is often omitted and this must not be. His name must be spoken because it is like perfume being poured out upon the horrid stench of the world. (See Song of Solomon 1:3.) Some have gone as far as to imitate the anointing of God. Imitators of the anointing operate illegally in the realm of the spirit assessing demonic wisdom, passing it off as the power of God.

This false anointing that flows from the mouths of the wicked and into the ears of equally wicked hearers has caused a horrific odor throughout the body of Christ. It is sent by the enemy to mimic the movements of God in order to confuse the flock. The counterfeit anointing circulating causes the people of God to "turn away from the faith, giving attention to deluding and seducing spirits and doctrines that demons teach, through the hypocrisy and pretensions of liars whose consciences are seared." (See 1 Timothy 4:1–2.)

Jesus Christ, the Messiah, is the Anointed One. In the Hebrew, *Messiah* is *Machiach*, and it is from *Machiach* that we get the word *mashach*[3], which means "anointing." Jesus is the source of our anointing as Christians. It is through relationship with Him that we pick up His fragrance; it is through relationship with Him that we are anointed. This means that we should have no anointing outside of Jesus. It also means that anything tapped into outside of Him is from a deceiving spirit that originated with Satan. The determining factor as to whether or not we are flowing in the true anointing is as simple as determining who our head is, because in the Book of Exodus, we learn that the anointing flows from the head down.

> But you have been anointed by [you hold a sacred appointment from, you have been given an unction from] the Holy One, and you all know [the Truth] or you know all things....But as for you, the anointing (the sacred appointment, the unction) which you received from Him abides [permanently] in you; [so] then you have no need that anyone should instruct you. But just as His anointing teaches you concerning everything and is true and is no falsehood, so you must abide in (live in, never depart from) Him [being rooted in Him, knit to Him], just as [His anointing] has taught you [to do].
>
> —1 JOHN 2:20, 27

A spirit of delusion as it relates to the anointing has caused many to misunderstand and lose sight of what truly constitutes it. Some have confused the true operation of the anointing with personalities and performances. "For certain men have crept in stealthily [gaining entrance secretly by a side door]. Their doom was predicted long ago, ungodly (impious, profane) persons who pervert the grace (the spiritual blessing and favor) of our God into lawlessness *and* wantonness *and* immorality, and disown *and* deny our sole Master and Lord, Jesus Christ (the Messiah, the Anointed One)" (Jude 1:4). Those with poisonous natures have obtained highly recognized platforms, leading the multitudes to hell. And like those who purchase counterfeit cologne, we have become sufficed by presentation alone. We are no longer concerned about what an individual is made of and have become more concerned with stage presence. It was the apostle Paul who said in First Corinthians 2:1 "as for myself, brethren, when I came to you, I did not come proclaiming to you the testimony and evidence or mystery and secret of God [concerning what He has done through Christ for the salvation of men] in lofty words of eloquence or human philosophy and wisdom."

Apostle Paul warned the people of Corinth not to become entrapped by long-winded, well-articulated sermons. If there is no power evident, then the ending is the same as its beginning—futile, fruitless, and worthless. We must not be enticed and led astray by the semantics and eloquence of men who appear to be of great stature, education, and position. Because while we are impressed with those things, God chooses less "qualified" individuals like Moses, Jeremiah, and the apostle Paul to speak on His behalf. God chooses the foolish things of the world to confound the wise.

Many make generalized statements such as, "that service was anointed," or "she has a great anointing." However, much of what had been witnessed was not the anointing in operation, but renegades in the spirit igniting strange fires. We reduce the anointing to goose bumps and being "slain in the spirit," when demonic organizations around the world conjure the exact same manifestations. Satan is a master of illusions but is unoriginal. He does not have the ability to create; he can only steal and counterfeit what God has already instituted. With that said, we have to be cognizant of what spirit were being slain in because if we arise the very same way we were before we went down, the Spirit of God was not in operation, but a deluding spirit of entertainment.

THE APOTHECARY

> Then take the anointing oil and pour it on his head and anoint him....Then you shall take part of the blood that is on the altar, and of the anointing oil, and sprinkle it upon Aaron and his garments and on his sons and their garments; and he and his garments and his sons and their garments shall be sanctified *and* made holy....The holy garments of Aaron shall pass to his descendants who succeed him, to be anointed in them and to be consecrated *and* ordained in them.

—EXODUS 29:7, 21, 29

The holy anointing oil was used to anoint Aaron and his sons and was symbolic of them being set apart and consecrated unto the Lord. The priests were to have the scent of God and to spread the knowledge of Him to others. Only qualified individuals, those set aside by God, were permitted to wear it. The Hebrew word meaning "to perfume" or "to prepare spices or a compound of spices" is the same as the word *apothecary*—from the Latin word *apothecarius*, meaning a "shopkeeper." Today, it is generally defined as "a health professional trained in the art of preparing and dispensing drugs."

From the biblical perspective, an apothecary was someone who prepared the holy anointing oil and incense. There was an *art* to this preparation, which denotes a certain grandeur and craft involved in its process. It was meticulous, well thought out, and

executed with exactness, precision, and excellence—
not done haphazardly. Thus an apothecary was one
who was skilled and trained. Among Moses'
responsibilities as prophet and priest, he was also
noted as an apothecary, perfumer, or a supervisor of
apothecaries. As an apothecary, Moses was given
hefty responsibilities. Ecclesiastes 10:1 says:

> Dead flies cause the ointment of the perfumer
> to putrefy [and] send forth a vile odor; so
> does a little folly [in him who is valued for
> wisdom] outweigh wisdom and honor.

Flies represent the works of demonic influences
employed by the "lord of the flies," Satan. As leaders
and members in the body of Christ, we are the
perfumers or apothecaries. And while we are
responsible for watching the oil—symbolic of the
anointing—and insuring that it is not tainted with
flies, the very hearts of many Christian apothecaries
have become infested with flies themselves. With
tainted anointings, leaders have been guilty of
contaminating members of the body by speaking
forth fifth into ears across the nation. If the head is
sick, the whole body is.

As God's supervisor of spices, Moses was also
given highly specific instructions on what
the holy anointing oil should consist of. Exodus
30:22–25 says:

> Moreover the LORD spake unto Moses,
> saying, Take thou also unto thee principal
> spices, of pure myrrh five hundred shekels,
> and of sweet cinnamon half so much, even
> two hundred and fifty shekels, and of sweet
> calamus two hundred and fifty shekels, and of
> cassia five hundred shekels, after the shekel of
> the sanctuary, and of oil olive an hin: and thou

> shalt make it an oil of holy ointment, an
> ointment compound after the art of the
> apothecary: it shall be an holy anointing oil.

Precision was important because any extra
ingredient added or taken away would cause a
perversion of the oil. If it was altered in any way, it
would not be considered the holy anointing oil but a
cheapened, counterfeit version. Thus, anything other
than what God has ordained as the anointing is
nothing more than an imposter. Exodus 30:31-33
says:

> And say to the Israelites, This is a holy
> anointing oil [symbol of the Holy Spirit],
> sacred to Me alone throughout your
> generations. It shall not be poured upon a
> layman's body, nor shall you make any other
> like it in composition; it is holy, and you shall
> hold it sacred. Whoever compounds any like it
> or puts any of it upon an outsider shall be cut
> off from his people.

God clearly instructed the children of Israel not to
attempt to duplicate the anointing oil. Likewise, we do
not have the liberty of adding to or subtracting from
what God has already ordained as holy. Leviticus
10:1–3 describes what happens when we proceed to
concoct our own version of the perfect instructions
of the Lord.

> And Nadab and Abihu, the sons of Aaron,
> each took his censer and put fire in it, and put
> incense on it, and offered strange and unholy
> fire before the Lord, as He had not
> commanded them. And there came forth fire
> from before the Lord and killed them, and
> they died before the Lord. Then Moses said to
> Aaron, This is what the Lord meant when He
> said, I [and My will, not their own] will be

acknowledged as hallowed by those who come near Me, and before all the people I will be honored. And Aaron said nothing.

Nadab and Abihu, priests of God, had been anointed and set apart for His use. They knew what was required of them for their office, how to worship God, and how to prepare the sacrifice unto Him. However, forsaking what they knew, they chose not to perform the sacrifice according to God's instructions. Instead, they offered a strange fire not warranted by Him.

The word *strange* in this text above is *zuwr*[4], which means "to be harlotrous." This "strangeness" means "to commit adultery." Nadab and Abihu's fire was an adulterous, harlotrous fire before the Lord. As harlot steps outside of the boundaries of marital vows to pursue fleshly desires, Nadab and Abihu stepped outside of what constituted an acceptable sacrifice unto God. Their adulterous hearts manifested in acts of disobedience and rebellion. It was considered a profane act because it was the work of their own hands. The Amplified Bible uses the word *unauthorized*, meaning "illegal." Nadab and Abihu performed unauthorized, illegal movements that day.

In this hour, many strange fires are being ignited. While claiming to be "fresh fires," they are actually unauthorized and illegal in the realm of the spirit because God is not in them. When the Lord consumed a sacrifice, it was because He was pleased and approved of the offering. Instead of consuming Nadab and Abihu's sacrifice in acceptance, God consumed them in judgment because they dared to come near a holy God with the unholy works of their flesh. As a result of their waywardness, "fire went out from the LORD and devoured them, and they died before the Lord" (Lv. 10:2). We must learn from their error; disobedience leads to death.

We cannot approach God in any way that we please, neither can we offer up strange fires expecting Him to accept them. Those who claim to operate in the anointing but truly don't will be consumed by the works of their hands. Their foundation will be exposed, and only those whose true foundation is based upon the Rock will stand. Apostle Paul says it best in First Corinthians 3:12-17:

> But if anyone builds upon the Foundation, whether it be with gold, silver, precious stones, wood, hay, straw, The work of each [one] will become [plainly, openly] known (shown for what it is); for the day [of Christ] will disclose and declare it, because it will be revealed with fire, and the fire will test and critically appraise the character and worth of the work each person has done. If the work which any person has built on this Foundation [any product of his efforts whatever] survives [this test], he will get his reward. But if any person's work is burned up [under the test], he will suffer the loss [of it all, losing his reward], though he himself will be saved, but only as [one who has passed] through fire. Do you not discern and understand that you [the whole church at Corinth] are God's temple (His sanctuary), and that God's Spirit has His permanent dwelling in you [to be at home in you, collectively as a church and also individually]? If anyone does hurt to God's temple or corrupts it [with false doctrines] or destroys it, God will do hurt to him and bring him to the corruption of death and destroy him. For the

> temple of God is holy (sacred to Him) and
> that [temple] you [¹the believing church and its
> individual believers] are.

As I was sitting in my office one day, I noticed an irritating fly that not only flew but also hopped from location to location. I attempted to swat it several times only to find I was a second too late because it would then hop to another location. After several minutes of trying to swat this one tiny fly, I decided to study its pattern. I determined how long the fly remained in one particular location and approximated how far it would hop so that I could swat it as it landed. The Word of God instructs us "not be ignorant and to know the pattern (devices) of the enemy (2 Cor. 2:11). In doing so, we will readily recognize false movements and counterfeit maneuvers. We would take note of those who hop from church to church, region to region, and nation to nation, orchestrating demonic movements and swat them as they land.

The Enemy counterfeits the anointing because he realizes that the power of God through purified vessels destroys his works. Flies have crept in, and we as the church must not be ignorant. As the body of Christ it is important that we recognize the true anointing if we are to exorcise the dead flies from our midst. Exodus 30 gives us an in-depth look at what the anointing of God truly looks like.

THE HOLY ANOINTING OIL

> Moreover the LORD spake unto Moses,
> saying, Take thou also unto thee principal
> spices, of pure myrrh five hundred shekels,
> and of sweet cinnamon half so much, even

> two hundred and fifty shekels, and of sweet
> calamus two hundred and fifty shekels, and of
> cassia five hundred shekels, after the shekel of
> the sanctuary, and of oil olive an hin: and thou
> shalt make it an oil of holy ointment, an
> ointment compound after the art of the
> apothecary: it shall be an holy anointing oil.
>
> —EXODUS 30:22–25, KJV

500 SHEKELS OF MYRRH

Myrrh, cherished as precious oil during biblical times, was a highly valued commodity in trade. It was used by the children of God to anoint sacred vessels of the Jewish temple and was also one of the three gifts given by the Magi to Jesus Christ when they paid tribute to Him. In the Book of Esther, it was used for purification purposes to beautify those who were to be presented before King Ahasurerus. In fact, it was a requirement of the law that the wives and concubines be purified and beautiful. Esther 2:12 says:

> Now when the turn of each maiden came to
> go in to King Ahasuerus, after the regulations
> for the women had been carried out for
> twelve months--since this was the regular
> period for their beauty treatments, six months
> with oil of myrrh and six months with sweet
> spices and perfumes and the things for the
> purifying of the women.

Myrrh is mentioned as the first ingredient in the holy anointing oil because we must first be purified before walking in untainted power. As Esther was required to be cleansed prior to sitting before the king, so must we as Christians be purified before we qualify as legitimate, effective, and powerful vessels of the anointing. It is when we sit before the King, in His Presence, that we are anointed so that our fragrance will fill the atmosphere of the world. (See Song of Solomon 1:12.)Any anointing accessed outside of being in the Presence of the King is unlawful. Anyone claiming to flow in the anointing and have not been with God are illegal rogues in the spirit.

Not only was myrrh used for purification purposes, but John 19:39–40 reveals that it was used to anoint the body of Jesus at the time of His burial. This is symbolic of us, as Christians, putting to death our old ways. We cannot be dead to sin and remain alive to old passions. It is to be understood that because Jesus died for our sins, we no longer have a life, but it is now the Christ who lives through us. If the Messiah, the Anointed One, lives in us, then we have an obligation to continuously allow sin to be put to death. Romans 8:13 says:

> For if you live according to [the dictates of] the flesh, you will surely die. But if through the power of the [Holy] Spirit you are [habitually] putting to death (making extinct, deadening) the [evil] deeds prompted by the body, you shall [really and genuinely] live forever.

250 SHEKELS OF SWEET CINNAMON

Cinnamon, the second ingredient of the holy anointing oil, is noted for its sweet permeating fragrance. *Bosem*[5] is the Hebrew word for *sweet* and it means "to be fragrant." The Hebrew word for cinnamon is *qinnamon*[6] which means "to stand erect." As the body of Christ, if we are to emit a sweet and savory fragrance to a world that is dying and decaying, we must stand erect (upright) in God. We must stand, being the righteous and living holy lives that are pleasing to Him. Once we exhibit these characteristics, our sweet fragrance will permeate the world around us.

> Therefore be imitators of God [copy Him and follow His example], as well-beloved children [imitate their father]. And walk in love, [esteeming and delighting in one another] as Christ loved us and gave Himself up for us, a slain offering and sacrifice to God [for you, so that it became] a sweet fragrance. But immorality (sexual vice) and all impurity [of lustful, rich, wasteful living] or greediness must not even be named among you, as is fitting and proper among saints (God's consecrated people). Let there be no filthiness (obscenity, indecency) nor foolish and sinful (silly and corrupt) talk, nor coarse jesting, which are not fitting or becoming; but instead voice your thankfulness [to God]. For be sure of this: that no person practicing sexual vice or impurity in thought or in life, or one who is covetous [who has lustful desire for the property of others and is greedy for gain]--for he [in effect] is an idolater--has any inheritance in the kingdom of Christ and of God.
>
> —EPHESIANS 5:1–5

250 SHEKELS OF SWEET CALAMUS

Calamus, also known as sweet cane, is a fragrant cane whose root is highly prized as a spice because of its healing properties. The calamus extraction process is one that is delicate and time consuming. First, there must be a collection of healthy roots because that is where the oil is extracted from. Thus, as Christians, in order to operate in the true anointing, we must have healthy roots. It is imperative that we are rooted and grounded in God because our anointing flows from our Source who is Jesus the Anointed One. (See Colossians 2:7.) The second step of extracting the oil is the purification stage. In this stage imperfections are removed from the calamus prior to processing it further. Likewise, we must allow the Word of God to continuously purify us so that the impurities and imperfections of sin will be removed from our lives.

Because of its tedious extraction process and highly medicinal properties, calamus was also very expensive. So it also speaks of cost. In other words, the true anointing of God will cost something. Isaiah 43:24 says:

> You have not bought Me sweet cane with money, or satiated Me with the fat of your sacrifices. But you have only burdened Me with your sins; you have wearied Me with your iniquities.

Because of the expense of the sweet calamus, the children of Israel chose to leave it out of their offering to God. They decided to omit what would cost them and continued to burden God by remaining in sin. Much like us today, the children of Israel gave God only what they felt like giving.

We live in a time where even professing Christians want something for nothing. Many want to be considered the "next big name" and to be used "mightily of God," but in reality, they are spiritual weaklings who don't want to pay the cost. We want an easy way to the power of God, but there is no easy way. There is only the right way and there is a price to be paid. David was not considered a man after God's own heart because he was perfect or that he always pleased God in his actions. On the contrary, he was a lying, murderous adulterer. First Chronicles 21:24–27 gives some insight into what pleases God.

> And King David said to Ornan, No, but I will pay the full price. I will not take what is yours for the Lord, nor offer burnt offerings which cost me nothing. So David gave to Ornan for the site 600 shekels of gold by weight. And David built there an altar to the Lord and offered burnt offerings and peace offerings and called upon the Lord; and He answered him by fire from heaven upon the altar of burnt offering. Then the Lord commanded the [avenging] angel, and he put his sword back into its sheath.

Many today use David's sin and weakness as an excuse to continue falling into the same sin, but it is to be understood that while David sinned, he also paid greatly for his sins. (See 2 Samuel 12.) David was a man after God's heart because he knew exactly what to do when he failed Him; he repented and *turned* from his sins. He also sacrificed to God and did not attempt to rob Him.

We are a generation that robs God. The word *sacrifice* causes us to cringe, when it is meant to be done willfully out of gratitude to the Lord. For the most part, when the children of Israel sacrificed, it was done cheerfully. They gave their very best to God and it was always costly.

In the gospel of Luke, Jesus says, "If any man wills to come after Me, let him deny himself, take up his cross daily, and follow Me" (Luke 9:23). Often the words "take up your cross" is associated with voluntary suffering—disease, financial lack, or hardship. But in actuality, death by crucifixion was a cruel, agonizing, and degrading way to die. The crosses were often visible upon a hill where surrounding towns could witness them at their lowest. The visibility of the crosses was an effort to humiliate the cross bearers, exposing them to public mockery and clamoring. In essence, those condemned to the cross had to carry their embarrassing, degrading, painful instrument of death upon his back.

In Palestinian times, following Jesus meant living in ways that directly opposed the Roman government. For us, as Christians, it means opposing the darkness of the world with the light of truth living on the inside of us. In doing so, we may be subjected to embarrassment and pain. We may be called heretics, yet we are to count it all joy when we fall into various trials for the sake of Jesus (James 1:2).

Jesus Christ who was fully man and fully God endured humiliation, torment, beatings, and mocking. He suffered an agonizing death. He could have called down legions of angels at any given moment, yet He despised the shame for the joy that was set before Him, He endured the cross (Heb. 12:2). What do you pursue most—your interests or God's glory? Self-denial is the voluntary action of resisting and desisting from everything that does not bring glory to God. Self-denial includes removing yourself from every activity, organization, club, and friend that denies Jesus. Can you let go of every costly thing that is inconsistent with living a holy lifestyle? Is your heart screaming, "Your kingdom come; Your will be done?" If the almighty God sacrificed and gave to us His very best, if God gave to us what cost Him—His darling Son—who are we to give anything less than our very best? Do not be deceived, Jesus commands those who follow Him to allow their flesh to be put to death so that He can be revealed in us to a world that needs the breath of life.

500 SHEKELS OF CASSIA

The Hebrew word for cassia is *qiddah*[7], which is similar to the word meaning "to bow down" or "to pay homage." *Homage* refers to honoring another by bending low in deep reverence. What greater example of humility do we know than that of Jesus Christ our Savior? Not only was He lowly and humble, He honored the Father in everything that He did. Why? John 8:54 says, "If I honor myself, my honor is nothing: it is my Father that honoreth me; of whom ye say, that he is your God" (KJV).

As anointed vessels of God, we are to be marked by humility. The humble individual is very much aware of his lowly place in position to an almighty and holy God. This individual knows that the highest place is at the feet of God. Those marked by humility have one purpose and one purpose alone and that is to see the will of God manifested in the earth as it is in heaven. Colossians 2:18–19 says:

> Do not let anyone who delights in false humility and the worship of angels disqualify you. Such a person also goes into great detail about what they have seen; they are puffed up with idle notions by their unspiritual mind. They have lost connection with the head, from whom the whole body, supported and held together by its ligaments and sinews, grows as God causes it to grow.
>
> —NIV

There is a notable absence of humility among leaders in the body of Christ today. Actually, many carry a false sense of humility because in appearance, they are meek, but upon their hearts and around their necks, they wear pride. The gaining of fans, producing television programs, and making appearances have taken the place of God inside of their hearts. Their desire is not to win souls but to obtain publicity. As a result, they have become idols in the hearts of the masses.

A HIN OF OLIVE OIL

The production of olive oil is a long, tedious process of pressing, scrapping, and pushing. First, the olives are checked for condition and sorted according to their maturation. The maturation level influences the acidity level of the oil. Any leaves and twigs still adhering to them are removed.

Likewise, the production of the anointing is not an overnight process. If we are to house the anointing, the Holy Spirit must be allowed to conduct a thorough check of our hearts with permission to remove everything in us that is unlike God. The level of our maturity determines the level of anointing that God flows through our lives. *Acidity* is the amount of free fatty acids that is in the olive oil. The less acid there is, the better the quality of the oil; the lower the acidity, the better the quality and taste. This part of the process for us as possible carriers of the anointing suggests that the removal of bitterness and other impurities is imperative to ensure high-quality anointing. If impurities remain in our lives then our flesh will surely contaminate it.

The next phase in the production of olive oil is milling. The word *mill* means "to grind, shape, sharpen, or refine with friction." It further means "to crush, pulverize, or reduce by friction, especially by rubbing between two hard surfaces." In order for the true anointing to come upon our lives, we will be beaten by the world, often feeling as though we are between a rock and a hard place, so to speak. It is not a comfortable place and as a result, many won't allow God to put them into the oven. They hate the fire but at the same time claim to operate in it. If we have never gone through anything, how can we be effective ministers in the kingdom of God. Friction will be caused in our lives in order to refine us, but it must be allowed in order to grow and to mature us in the anointing.

Next, the olives are washed in cold water and drained, before being crushed to break up the tissues and release the oil. This can be done by simultaneously cutting, shearing, and rubbing while heat is applied to encourage the oil to flow freely. The truly anointed individual must be emptied and drained of everything that is unlike God. Those things that hinder the flow of the anointing must be removed in order for it to be released into other's lives uncontaminated.

Furthermore, in order for the hindrances of the anointing to surface, we will be "(pressed) on every side [troubled and oppressed in every way], but not cramped or crushed; we suffer embarrassments and are perplexed and unable to find a way out, but not driven to despair; we are pursued (persecuted and hard driven), but not deserted [to stand alone]; we are struck down to the ground, but never struck out and destroyed" (2 Cor. 4:8–9). The anointing can only be smelled when the vessel that houses it is broken. The true anointing rests upon those who have laid down their lives realizing that they no longer have a life.

In a vision, I saw a corroding dead body being sprayed heavily with fragrant perfume. After which, I heard the Lord say, "What good is it for a dead man to wear perfume? Many of My children are walking around in deadness—deadness in their worship, deadness in their hearts, deadness in their lives. Church attendance is at an all-time high, but where is the true church? The Word of God is alive, fragrant, and appealing. But many in high places are preaching a putrid gospel, speaking in My name and I have not spoken. Enough! They don't have the Spirit of God but a spirit of Amnon—a greedy, prideful spirit—and it stinks. A dead rotten corroding stench attempts to overpower the sweetness of My testimony. Therefore, shame will grace many who spoke words from dark counsel and their flesh, attaching My name to them. The body of Christ has been suffering a tremendous loss, the loss of authentic voices who speak on behalf of God. Yes, there are some prophets who speak what it is they hear, but counterfeiters corrupt and infest the lives of My children with corrupted, inauthentic smear. My name has been defiled. There are some on the forefront who do not belong. They put up a façade for sons of men and make a mockery out of My words. They parade around only to be seen and struggle with truth. They live their lives as if there is no God. Whom do they fear?" *May 15, 2009*

Many who are spiritually dead attempt to mimic the fragrance of Christ, but once the smell of their cheap, counterfeit cologne dissipates, the stench of the world is exposed. It must be understood that the fragrance of Christ is often imitated by imposters, but it is deadly to duplicate. Soon, there will be a great separation. God is going to separate the sheep from the goats, the wheat from the tares, and the authentic from the counterfeit. No longer will these individuals operating in a counterfeit anointing have the ability to entertain the saints with pulpit shenanigans. As we grow closer to God, He is getting ready to release the sweet smell of spiritual discernment upon His body like never before. First John 2:27 says:

> But as for you, the anointing (the sacred appointment, the unction) which you received from Him abides [permanently] in you; [so] then you have no need that anyone should instruct you. But just as His anointing teaches you concerning everything and is true and is no falsehood, so you must abide in (live in, never depart from) Him [being rooted in Him, knit to Him], just as [His anointing] has taught you [to do].

By the anointing, the ability to distinguish between the real and the counterfeit is second nature. The time is approaching when the true anointing will be demanded and if there is no anointing, many will no longer be demanded.

> For behold, the Lord, the Lord of hosts, is taking away from Jerusalem and from Judah the stay and the staff [every kind of prop], the whole stay of bread and the whole stay of water, the mighty man and the man of war, the judge *and* the [professional] prophet, the one who foretells by divination and the old man, the captain of fifty and the man of rank, the counselor and the expert craftsman and the skillful enchanter....And it shall come to pass that instead of the sweet odor of spices there shall be the stench of rottenness; and instead of a girdle, a rope; and instead of well-set hair, baldness; and instead of a rich robe, a

girding of sackcloth; and searing [of captives by the scorching heat] instead of beauty.

—ISAIAH 3:1–3, 24

PART I

THE
SPIRITS
of
HARLOTRY

2

THE SPIRIT *of* HARLOTRY

Sauntering through the street near the [loose woman's] corner; and he went the way to her house In the twilight, in the evening; night black and dense was falling [over the young man's life]. And behold, there met him a woman, dressed as a harlot and sly and cunning of heart. She is turbulent and willful; her feet stay not in her house....I have perfumed my bed with myrrh, aloes, and cinnamon....With much justifying and enticing argument she persuades him, with the allurements of her lips she leads him [to overcome his conscience and his fears] and forces him along.

—PROVERBS 7:8–11, 17, 21

THE ENTERTAINMENT INDUSTRY and, for some, firsthand experience has imprinted images into our minds as to how a harlot looks and smells as well as what she does. A harlot is typically envisioned as a young woman dressed provocatively in tightly fitted clothing, tawdry jewelry, and sky high stilettos. Her face is painted in pale foundation, bright red lipstick, heavy blush, and powder blue eye shadow. With a cigarette pursed between her lips, she leans into an anonymous car window and seductively gives a prospective client a rundown of her services. She reeks of cheap counterfeit perfume, alcohol, and of her many indiscretions. Although statistics reveal otherwise, she is viewed as the hub of sexually transmitted disease. She is judged as the disease ridden smudge that dirties up our otherwise "clean and wholesome" society.

While this description is accurate in some instances, it is definitely not conclusive. The International Standard Bible Encyclopedia describes the harlot[8] as an "unchaste woman, married or unmarried, or a prostitute." A prostitute is one who "offers up oneself or one's talent for unworthy purposes."

With this definition in mind, it is evident that prostitution is not limited to sexual acts alone. Whatever takes place in the natural realm is only a manifestation of what is happening or has happened in the realm of the spirit. If there is natural prostitution, then there is also spiritual prostitution. So, spiritual prostitution or harlotry is the offering up of oneself at all costs in exchange for selfish gain. It is abandoning God's statutes for what the world has to offer; it is prostituting the anointing and gifts He has entrusted us with as His children. It is taking God given gifts and misusing them for unworthy purposes.

Thus, it is not necessary to travel to a local street corner, brothel, or sleazy motel to find a harlot. It would seem that the probability of locating a harlot is much easier than we may realize. Some harlots will not be found on dark, dingy street corners selling sex; spiritual harlots stand upon beautifully decorated platforms selling the Word of God. They do not dress promiscuously, but are robed in priestly white garments and three-piece suits. Spiritual harlots are those whose adornment is merely outward because inwardly are dead men's bones. They outwardly profess holiness and righteousness, but are adulterers at heart.

Many believe that Psalm 38 is a psalm of distress written by David while suffering from a venereal disease as a result of his adulterous acts with Bathsheba. Verse 5 discusses the sores which he had in his loins; they were corrupted and had a terrible stench. Much like David, God's people have become facilitators of disease. However, spiritual harlots do not carry disease in their physical bodies; they have heart disease and are guilty of spreading corruption throughout the body of Christ. With their highly charismatic nature, eloquent speech, and adulterous hearts, they infect their listeners causing sores and blemishes upon the body.

The Hebrew word for "harlot" is *kadasha*. It is interesting that the Hebrew word for "holy" is *kadusha* which means "set apart, separate, sacred, and free from uncleanness." How could two words that are obviously the exact opposite of each other look so similar in the Hebrew? Taking a closer look at both words, we find that they each deal with boundaries. For example, God is not bound by time or space. He does not live within the boundaries of this world, He created them for us. Nothing in the world has the ability to affect or change Him. He is and forever will be holy.

Similarly, harlots live outside of the boundaries of descent and normal society and are deemed unholy.

This is the tragedy that is happening around us today. We are to be betrothed to the Lord as a church, but have been guilty of stepping outside of the bounds of holiness and slipping into harlotry. There is a fine line between holiness and wickedness.

In a vision, I saw dark walls tightly compressed around a woman as she walked down a narrow hallway. Down the narrow path was bright light emitting. "Narrow is the road that leads to life" (Matt. 7:13). We cannot afford to slip into harlotry at the sake of living holy lives before God. While the topic of holiness is shunned and viewed as dated, the day is coming when it will grace the lips of those truly called by God. They will revert to the days of old where holiness is not only the center of sermons, but also the center of the lives of those who preach it. Holiness is most certainly needed to break spiritual harlotry within the body of Christ.

GOMER, WIFE OF HARLOTRY

> When the Lord first spoke with and through Hosea, the Lord said to him, Go, take to yourself a wife of harlotry and have children of [her] harlotry, for the land commits great whoredom by departing from the Lord.
>
> —HOSEA 1:2

The marriage between Hosea and Gomer was symbolic of Israel's whorish attitude and indifference toward God in their union. Hosea's consistent and persistent chasing after his estranged wife was representative of the heart of God and His undying love for those who did not love Him and chose harlotry in His stead. It is to be understood that in the text above, Gomer is never technically referred to as a harlot or as a prostitute. Hosea was called to marry a "wife of harlotry." Thus, Gomer was not a harlot when she and Hosea married. She was a married woman who chose to step outside of the boundaries of marriage. She slipped into harlotry to pursue the desires of her wicked heart only *after* she and Hosea were married. When outlying contributing factors presented themselves to Gomer, she was found unfaithful because there was sickness in her heart that lied dormant until it was awakened by opportunity. After which, the harlotry deeply embedded inside of her heart manifested in her actions. Matthew 5:27–28 says:

> You have heard that it was said, You shall not commit adultery. But I say to you that everyone who so much as looks at a woman with evil desire for her has already committed adultery with her in his heart.

Jeremiah 17:9 says:

> The heart is deceitful above all things, and it is exceedingly perverse and corrupt and severely, mortally sick! Who can know it [perceive, understand, be acquainted with his own heart and mind]?

The children of Israel rightfully belonged to God but began to play the harlot with neighboring countries engaging in paganism. They became so engrossed into the culture of the idolaters—listening to their music, eating their food, and worshiping their idols—that their hearts became infected. They were heartsick. Similarly, many within the body of Christ have become accustomed to the ways of the world and their patterns, becoming chameleons of harlotry.

> My people [habitually] ask counsel of their
> [senseless] wood [idols], and their staff [of
> wood] gives them oracles and instructs them
> for the spirit of harlotry has led them astray
> and they have played the harlot, withdrawing
> themselves from subjection to their God.

> —HOSEA 4:12

The phrase "led astray" means "to wander as well
as "to be deceived, seduced, and ultimately led to
ruin." It means to "remove oneself from under the
influence and authority of God and sneak off into the
influence of another spirit." It depicts a woman
sneaking off to be with her lover.

The word *spirit* as it is used in the text above
describes a "strong domineering demonic force
that overshadows and drives an individual into
slavery." The spirit of harlotry is a principality that
specializes in causing hearts that were once devoted
to God to turn away from Him and toward the
counsel of demons. Becoming enticed into alternative
sinful lifestyles, they become slaves to sin. Like
Gomer, Israel allowed the spirit of harlotry to lead
them instead of the Spirit of God. The spirit of
harlotry is at the core of the great falling away spoken
of in 2 Thessalonians 2:3–4, which says:

> Let no one deceive or beguile you in any way,
> for that day will not come except the apostasy
> comes first [unless the predicted great falling
> away of those who have professed to be
> Christians has come], and the man of
> lawlessness (sin) is revealed, who is the son of
> doom (of perdition),(Who opposes and exalts
> himself so proudly and insolently against and
> over all that is called God or that is
> worshiped, [even to his actually] taking his

seat in the temple of God, proclaiming that he himself is God.

Many are seduced into the arms of false doctrines of demons, by a compromised word and a false gospel.

CHILDREN OF HARLOTRY

> When the Lord first spoke with and through Hosea, the Lord said to him, Go, take to yourself a wife of harlotry and have children of [her] harlotry, for the land commits great whoredom by departing from the Lord.
>
> —HOSEA 1:2

Not only was Hosea called to take a wife of harlotry, but he was also called to father three children birthed in the midst of Gomer's harlotry. Hosea's children were testaments to the abominations that were taking place in Israel before the face of their Groom. The names of his children were prophetic and direct indicators of what God had in store for Israel if they did not turn and repent.

Jezreel, the first born of Gomer, was also the name of a city that was located in the middle or the heart of Israel. It was a place that was infested with harlotrous acts and bloodshed. Jezreel's name means "God scatters." The symbolism behind his name was not only descriptive of Israel's heart, but of their punishment as well. Their hearts were corrupt because wickedness was at their core. As a result, God would scatter them. The second child's name, Lo-ruhamah, means "not beloved" or "not having obtained mercy," and foretold of God's abandoning the nation because they had already abandoned Him in their hearts and deeds. God had shown Israel extravagant mercy, but they rejected Him choosing to be slaves of their desires.

Many are aware that God is a loving God. This is true, God extends mercy, but it's up to us to live holy and accept the mercy He freely gives. The third child was called Lo'Ammi, which means "not My people." This name reflected God's judgment upon the children of Israel because they continued to reject Him. It speaks aloud what was already implanted into the hearts and minds of those He once called His Bride—their decision to abandon God.

When we as children of God divorce Him for the world, we give birth to the wrath of God. Many don't like to discuss His wrath, but when we don't, we are in danger of creating a false understanding of who God truly is. Inside of God's love is His wrath. He cannot allow His children to live as harlots of the world unpunished because He disciplines those whom He loves. (See Hebrews 12:6.) His infinite love and mercy for His children is documented in Ezekiel 16:5–9, which says:

> No eye pitied you to do any of these things for you, to have compassion on you; but you were cast out in the open field, for your person was abhorrent and loathsome on the day that you were born. And when I passed by you and saw you rolling about in your blood, I said to you in your blood, Live! Yes, I said to you still in your natal blood, Live! I caused you [Israel] to multiply as the bud which grows in the field, and you increased and became tall and you came to full maidenhood and beauty; your breasts were formed and your hair had grown, yet you were naked and bare. Now I passed by you again and looked upon you; behold, you were

> maturing and at the time for love, and I
> spread My skirt over you and covered your
> nakedness. Yes, I plighted My troth to you
> and entered into a covenant with you, says the
> Lord, and you became Mine. Then I washed
> you with water; yes, I thoroughly washed away
> your [clinging] blood from you and I anointed
> you with oil.

God looked down and witnessed the newborn choking in its own blood—nearly dead and abandoned by unloving and wicked parents. He showed compassion and gave the newborn life. He washed away the stench of its blood and anointed it.

While the baby portrayed in the text above is Israel, it is also descriptive of how our Lord cares for us as His children. While we were yet sinners, rolling around in the filthiness of our own sin, Jesus went to the cross and gave His life so that we could have life. Because we are shaped in iniquity, He has offered to live through us, if allowed. Once we become His, we are washed and cleansed by His blood. Furthermore, He anoints us to accomplish the destiny and purpose He placed within us before the foundations of the earth. Ezekiel 16:10–14 continues:

> I clothed you also with embroidered cloth and
> shod you with [fine seal] leather; and I girded
> you about with fine linen and covered you
> with silk. I decked you also with ornaments
> and I put bracelets on your wrists and a chain
> on your neck. And I put a ring on your nostril
> and earrings in your ears and a beautiful
> crown upon your head! Thus you were decked
> with gold and silver, and your raiment was of
> fine linen and silk and embroidered cloth; you
> ate fine flour and honey and oil. And you
> were exceedingly beautiful and you prospered
> into royal estate. And your renown went forth

among the nations for your beauty, for it was perfect through My majesty and splendor which I had put upon you, says the Lord God.

The word embroidered is only used five times in the entire Bible. Three of those times it was mentioned was in reference to the tabernacle. It seems that embroidering was reserved for special tasks alone. It is a term that speaks of detail and fanciful design and is not merely sewing or stitching cloth. To embroider is to add embellishment and artistry. When one embroiders, one designs something intricately. Psalm 139:13–16 says:

> For You formed my inward parts; You covered me in my mother's womb. I will praise You, for I am fearfully and wonderfully made Marvelous are Your works, and that my soul knows very well. My frame was not hidden from You, when I was made in secret, and skillfully wrought in the lowest parts of the earth. Your eyes saw my substance, being yet unformed. And in Your book they all were written, the days fashioned for me, when as yet there were none of them.

To design is to conceive and fashion in the mind. It is a "thought out systematic plan with one purpose in mind, to create or execute in an artistic or highly skilled manner, to fashion." God knit together and designed a perfect plan for Israel and for us as His children. Not only did He knit us in our mother's womb, but He designed specific corporate and individual destinies for us. Our lives are elaborately furnished with rich apparel.

> I clothed you also with embroidered cloth and shod you with [fine seal] leather…

Badger skin was used to cover the furniture in the tabernacle, and thus it was a substance of rarity and great value. The fact that badger skin is used in the manufacturing of shoes implies that it is very strong and able to withstand harsh weather.

God gave Israel the ability to stand, remain durable, steadfast, and strong with the ability to last. God covered their path and blessed them so that wherever their feet treaded, they had the possibility to possess it. Their feet were covered to stand securely upon their high places. (See Psalm 40:2.) They were equipped with the ability to remain firm and to complete the task that God had given them, but they refused.

> ...and your raiment was of fine linen and silk and embroidered cloth...

Silk and linen were both used in the making of very fine fabrics. Linen was not only used in manufacture garments of the priests but also for shrouds, hangings, and other highly prized items. Linen represents righteousness and symbolizes purity, sincerity, and obedience. It represents a pure life submitted to God and His statutes. God stripped Israel of her filthy garments and placed upon her those befitting a bride but again, like a harlot, she stripped them off her back. Revelation 19:8 says:

> She has been permitted to dress in fine (radiant) linen, dazzling and white—for the fine linen is (signifies, represents) the righteousness (the upright, just, and godly living, deeds, and conduct, and right standing with God) of the saints (God's holy people).

As the body of Christ, we are permitted to dress in white linen, which is righteousness. However, like the children of Israel many of God's people have chosen to dress in leather skirts and stilettos instead of robes of righteousness.

> And I put a ring on your nostril and earrings in your ears and a beautiful crown upon your head! Thus you were decked with gold and silver.
>
> —EZEKIEL 16:12–13

As a groom slips a wedding ring onto the finger of his bride on their wedding day, so did God symbolically place upon Israel, a seal of their marital vows. His love for us is irreplaceable, it is inconceivable, yet lately unfaithfulness has begun to surface whenever opportunity knocks. We must not slip off our robes of righteousness to engage in the cheap thrills the Enemy attempts to lure us away with.

WICKED PARENTS

The amazing love God displays to His children is to be mimicked by His children. However, like Gomer, leaders controlled by the spirit of harlotry are only giving birth to children of harlotry. There is much to be said about spiritual parentage nowadays. And sadly, many who have not been called of the Lord, have self-appointed themselves as spiritual mothers and fathers. The result is the birthing of wickedness in the body of Christ. Ezekiel 16:1-3 says:

> Again the word of the Lord came to me, saying, Son of man, cause Jerusalem to know, understand, and realize her [idolatrous] abominations [that they] are disgusting, detestable, and shamefully vile. And say, Thus says the Lord God to Jerusalem [representing Israel]: Your [spiritual] origin and your birth

> are thoroughly Canaanitish; your [spiritual]
> father was an Amorite and your [spiritual]
> mother a Hittite.

The Amorites and the Hittites were known as the corrupt of the corrupt and in the text above, God reminded Jerusalem of where it was they came from. Even though they were nothing, born in sin and shaped in iniquity, God seeing their substance knew the potential they held as a nation as long as they remained faithful to Him. (See Psalm 139 and Psalm 51:5.) Ezekiel 16:4 says:

> And as for your birth, on the day you were born your navel cord was not cut, nor were you washed with water to cleanse you, nor rubbed with salt or swaddled with bands at all.

To keep the umbilical cord from rotting, a great deal of care and assistance is needed, yet we see in the verse above that the parent neglected to do so. Likewise, many self-professed "spiritual parents" are arising all over the globe with their own motives in mind. They are guilty of not taking proper care of newborns in Christ. As a result, rottenness is being birthed within the church.

Failure to cut the umbilical cord results in the baby remaining attached to its mother. False spiritual parents influenced by the spirit of harlotry have no desire to cut the naval cord, because they are controlling. Thus, many become "parents" in order to control every aspect of their spiritual children's lives and even worse, to ensure their "children" don't go any further than they have. These individuals are being used by the Enemy to stunt the growth of the body of Christ. Marked by jealousy and a spirit of competition, they often find themselves competing with the very ones they should nurture into proper development.

In the gospel of John, Jesus spoke to His disciples after they marveled at the miracles, signs, and wonders He'd performed, saying, "Greater works shall you do." Control and neglect is not the pattern of God. A true spiritual parent desires to see their child go further adding more to the kingdom of God for the glory of God. One of the reasons we are not seeing greater works is because newborns are being stifled and limited by those who are not called to parent them to begin with. The church building is not a holding ground for those with potential. It should be a center of training and development so the young in God are properly taught and then equipped to go into the world to fulfill the Great Commission. We must be careful of whom it is we are considering to be spiritual parents. We must make sure that God is at the center of the relationship, because if not, this will be evident in their walk as well as our own.

SALT

> And as for your birth, on the day you were born your navel cord was not cut, nor were you washed with water to cleanse you, nor rubbed with salt or swaddled with bands at all.
>
> —EZEKIEL 16:4

Even after the wicked parent neglected to cut the naval cord of the newborn, we see further neglect in that the baby was also not rubbed with salt. Salt is a powerful mineral used since ancient times in many cultures as a preservative, seasoning, and disinfectant. It was used to prevent corruption from the cutting of the naval cord and to strengthen the newborn, which would have been the case for the baby in the verse above.

Corruption is taking place in the church because the birthing of salt-less children is rapidly increasing. Because the wicked parents themselves are not seasoned with salt, they have no desire to properly care for those they claim to "birth out." They quote Matthew 5:13 "we are the salt of the earth," yet often times instead of being disinfectants, seasonings, and preservatives, they are responsible for spreading majority of the decay and infection to their newborns.

CHARACTERISTICS OF SALT

> All the heave offerings [the lifted-out and kept portions] of the holy things which the Israelites give to the Lord I give to you and to your sons and your daughters with you, as a continual debt forever. It is a covenant of salt [that cannot be dissolved or violated] forever before the Lord for you [Aaron] and for your posterity with you.
>
> —NUMBERS 18:19

> Ought ye not to know that the LORD God of Israel gave the kingdom over Israel to David forever, even to him and to his sons by a covenant of salt?
>
> —2 CHRONICLES 13:5

Salt is the one preservative that is pure and cannot be destroyed just at the covenant of God is pure and can't be destroyed. Thus, the word *salt* as it is used in God's covenant is symbolic of the durability of His Word, His faithfulness toward His Word, and the purity and incorruptibility of His Word. The Word of God is invaluable, because it is impervious. The Salt

71

Covenant provides a look into characteristics we as Christians should possess.

1. DURABILITY

Durability is "having stability, the ability to endure, the capability of withstanding decay, and the ability to perform." Salted Christians are stable and "those who (hesitates, doubts) is like the billowing surge out at sea that is blown hither and thither and tossed by the wind." (See James 1:6.)

Without durability, one does not have the ability to keep covenant or vows. They are easily blown away by waves of false doctrine. This is evident with Israel who lacked permanence; without difficulty they abandoned covenant with God to play the harlot. The lack of durability results in irresponsible Christians who are aimless and have no sense of stability. Salt less Christians are weak Christians who switch alliances the moment pressure arises. They are incapable of remaining dedicated to their beloved Bridegroom. Durability is imperative in order to take a stand against the wickedness in our midst, the wiles of Satan.

> Therefore, my beloved brethren, be firm (steadfast), immovable, always abounding in the work of the Lord [always being superior, excelling, doing more than enough in the service of the Lord], knowing and being continually aware that your labor in the Lord is not futile [it is never wasted or to no purpose].
>
> —1 CORINTHIANS 15:58

2. FAITHFULNESS

Genesis describes one of the most discussed and interpreted stories of the Bible, the story of Lot's wife. We know that Lot 's family was in the midst of escaping the wrath of God's judgment upon Sodom and Gomorrah because of their horrendous, abominable acts. As Lot and his family were being led away from what God abhorred, his wife looked back and was turned into a pillar of salt. While Lot's wife physically looked back with her eyes, it was only because her heart looked back first. Because, her heart had become sick and infested with Sodom and Gomorrah, a part of her still craved what God detested. Her unfaithful heart turned and made a choice that day, she chose the world. She had lost her taste and was good for nothing but to be thrown down and trampled underfoot by man. (See Matthew 5:13.)

Faithfulness is defined as "adhering firmly and devotedly, as to a person, cause, or idea; loyal." Without faithfulness marriages end, hearts turn, and covenants are broken. The lack of loyalty is why the children of Israel persistently strayed away and why Christians are falling for the seductive allure of the world. Unfaithful believers do not have the ability to follow God wholeheartedly. Just as Lot's wife was unable to let go of worldly attachments and was judged, if we are unable to shake the world's hold on us and are unable to remain faithful, we will likewise be judged.

> And if your eye causes you to stumble and sin, pluck it out! It is more profitable and wholesome for you to enter the kingdom of

God with one eye than with two eyes to be thrown into hell (Gehenna),Where their worm [which preys on the inhabitants and is a symbol of the wounds inflicted on the man himself by his sins] does not die, and the fire is not put out. For everyone shall be salted with fire. Salt is good (beneficial), but if salt has lost its saltness, how will you restore [the saltness to] it? Have salt within yourselves, and be at peace and live in harmony with one another.

—MARK 9:47-50

3. PURITY

And the men of the city said to Elisha, Behold, inhabiting of this city is pleasant, as my lord sees, but the water is bad and the locality causes miscarriage and barrenness [in all animals].He said, Bring me a new bowl and put salt [the symbol of God's purifying power] in it. And they brought it to him. Then Elisha went to the spring of the waters and cast the salt in it and said, Thus says the Lord: I [not the salt] have healed these waters; there shall not be any more death, miscarriage or barrenness [and bereavement] because of it.

—2 KINGS 2:19-21

Salt is also symbolic of purity and obedience. As the saints of God, we must be purified by the washing of the Word of God. Hearing and obeying the unadulterated Word of God is the only way we are washed clean. (See Ephesians 5:26.) It is the responsibility of the leader to present the gospel as written and it is the responsibility of us all to obey the Truth as it was given. However, the people of God have been spoon fed milk, when solid food is needed to prevent spiritual death.

In the body, salt is as important to humans as water or air. It regulates the water in the body and helps to maintain the normal volume of blood in the body. Salt is also necessary for the formation and proper function of nerve fibers, which carry impulses to and from the brain, and plays an important part in the digestion of food. It is essential in making the heart beat correctly[9].

We as leaders and followers of Christ must begin to regulate the watered down messages circulating in the body of Christ which is resulting in spiritual miscarriages and death. As God's apothecaries, we are responsible for protecting the anointing. Leaders must instruct their children in the way of purity and holiness, but they must first be shown. Our hearts will not beat for the Lord if we are impure.

4. VALUE

> You are the salt of the earth, but if salt has lost its taste (its strength, its quality), how can its saltness be restored? It is not good for anything any longer but to be thrown out and trodden underfoot by men.
>
> —MATTHEW 5:13

Value is defined as "the desirability of a thing, often in respect of some property such as usefulness or exchangeability; worth, merit or importance." Salt had great value in times past but even today, it has over 14,000 uses. We too, as Christians are valuable; but if we lose our flavor, like Lot's wife, we become worthless. Unfortunately, many of the young in God are devalued and counted as weak things by those considered of "higher rank."

In a dream, I saw children seated against walls inside of a church. Standing over them were older women who were obviously their teachers. A young girl sat holding her face as though she had just been struck, but upon further evaluation it was determined that she had actually been badly burned. When asked what happened to her, she looked up at the teacher in fear and quickly looked away, not answering. I knew that one of the leaders had burned the child. Grandiose in appearance and stature, the abusing leader looked to be an exceptional woman of God. She was dressed appropriately in priestly garments, but inside she was rotten to the core.

Eighty percent of prostitutes have been sexually abused as children. Having been devalued, typically, by someone they knew, the abused child accepted the abuse as the norm and began to live their lives matching the way they felt inside. Feeling worthless and unloved, they slipped into prostitution.

Not only does sexual, physical and emotional abuse exist, so does spiritual abuse. Many of the young in God are burned by their leaders in the church. Influenced by harlotrous leaders, they become intimidated and fearful, hiding behind the very people who abuse them. Having been demeaned for so long, abuse has become the norm and spiritual harlotry, their chosen path. Spiritual leaders with whom God has entrusted with His flock have been guilty of abusing those they are called to protect.

Ezekiel 16:4 also states that the newborn was not "swaddled." Swaddling aids with warmth and security. It helps the newborn to feel secure, preventing and protecting them from hurting themselves. In other words, often times the new in God are not provided with the warmth, security, and reliability of loving parents. As a result, they become self-destructive in the kingdom of God.

In another dream, I watched a woman inside of an activity center where a variety of activities were taking place, including swimming. She wanted to swim badly but could not find swimming gear anywhere and there was absolutely no one there who would aid her in her search. Everyone was preoccupied with their own concerns and less than concerned about hers. Matthew 25:26–30 says:

> But his master answered him, You wicked and lazy and idle servant! Did you indeed know that I reap where I have not sowed and gather [grain] where I have not winnowed? Then you should have invested my money with the bankers, and at my coming I would have received what was my own with interest. So take the talent away from him and give it to the one who has the ten talents. For to everyone who has will more be given, and he will be furnished richly so that he will have an abundance; but from the one who does not have, even what he does have will be taken away. And throw the good-for-nothing servant into the outer darkness; there will be weeping and grinding of teeth.

Swimming in this dream, represents flowing in the gifts and talents of God. Many are stifled and not allowed to use their God-given talents. Furthermore, they do not know how to operate in them because gifts are not being cultivated by those in leadership. There is a notable absence of authentic spiritual discipleship. Because of this lack, believers walk about aimlessly within the body, not knowing where to turn or what to do. The spirit of harlotry causes many to become useless within the kingdom of God.

The young in God, His newborns, must be valued and treated with respect. As I state quite often throughout this book, it is God Himself who uses the weak things to bring low those who profess to be wise. (See 1 Corinthians 1:27.) The weak things have been forgotten by man but remembered and valued by God. This is what I heard God say:

"Judgment is coming upon false prophets who stand in holy places and defile My Name...Who prophesy in My name and have not heard from Me, who lead My precious flock astray, who seek out to destroy My Name in the eyes of those I love, who stand upon their high places and burn incense to the gods in their hearts. They birth corruption; they birth strife, and division among My children. They birth death and worship dead things. Their words have no life because I Am not in them. They speak death into the lives of My people and plant seeds of corruption into their wombs. I tell you, this will stop. As the fish I prepared for Jonah, so has man allowed their greed to swallow up My children. They rob them of their purity and innocence, leaving them ravished and degraded. They are causing My children, My own to be ostracized and spiritually poor, aloof from Me. Shame on them, for judgment soon arises and shall shine upon their faces as My glory should have. Their greed is a noose around their necks that will render death. The greed for power and wealth has been their lot. I Am far from their lists of pleasure. They worship their valuables, which are of no value. Their possessions have become gods to them, while My poor roam the streets hungry, thirsty, and devastated by sons of men. I tell you that the day comes and it will not tarry that their parties will become as funerals. Their songs will become dirges. Their laughter will become tears. Their joy at the expense of My children shall be their death. Their persistent sin will cause them to be without My voice. The voice they ignored when I pleaded with them to love Me, the voice they ignored when I asked them to truthfully guide My flock, the very voice they ignored when they stood upon their high places and burned incense to their gods. As the fish I prepared for Jonah vomited him up, so shall I spew them from My mouth. The day comes and it will not tarry." *June 1, 2009*

When leaders of God persistently mishandle God's flock and ignore His voice, they become desensitized to His voice. Sooner or later God will give them over to their wicked desires, which ultimately leads to death.

THE FALL OF WICKED SPIRITUAL LEADERS

> But you trusted in and relied on your own beauty and were unfaithful to God and played the harlot [in idolatry] because of your renown, and you poured out your fornications upon anyone who passed by [as you worshiped the idols of every nation which prevailed over you] and your beauty was his. And you took some of your garments and made for yourself gaily decorated high places or shrines and played the harlot on them-- things which should not come and that which should not take place. You did also take your fair jewels and beautiful vessels of My gold and My silver which I had given you and made for yourself images of men, and you played the harlot with them; And you took

79

> your embroidered garments and covered them
> and set My oil and My incense before them.
> My bread also which I gave you--fine flour
> and oil and honey with which I fed you--you
> have even set it before the idols for a sweet
> odor. Thus it was, says the Lord God.
>
> —EZEKIEL 16:15–19

Many leaders today have followed the pattern of the children of Israel. Falling into the delusions of the enemy, they sit upon high places and have allowed fame to warp their minds. They have been deceived into believing that they are untouchable. God set them upon high places so that people would be drawn to Him, but leaders have betrayed God and are concerned only with seeking their own glory. It is no longer God that is seen but the flesh of men. Ezekiel 16:20–25 says:

> Moreover, you have taken your sons and your
> daughters whom you have borne to Me, and
> you have sacrificed them [to your idols] to be
> destroyed. Were your harlotries too little, That
> you have slain My children and delivered
> them up, in setting them apart and causing
> them to pass through the fire for [your idols]?
> And in all your abominations and idolatrous
> whoredoms you have not [earnestly]
> remembered the days of your youth when you
> were naked and bare, rolling about in your
> natal blood. And after all your wickedness--
> Woe, woe to you! says the Lord God-- You
> have built also for yourself a vaulted chamber
> (brothel) and have made a high place [of idol
> worship] in every street. At every crossway
> you built your high place [for idol worship]
> and have made your beauty an abomination
> [abhorrent, loathsome, extremely disgusting,
> and detestable]; and you have made your body

available to every passerby and multiplied
your [idolatry and spiritual] harlotry.

I leave you with a word the Lord gave to me:
"Falling leader, when I found you, you were
wounded. Yes, you were choking in your own blood.
I caused you to live. I removed your reproach. I
allowed you to drink from My wisdom, and you grew
in knowledge. You even matured and you developed
in Me, though even with wisdom, you lacked depth. I
covered your lack, and I hid your shame. I exchanged
your shame for My glory. Yes, the riches of My
presence covered you and you were nurtured. I loved
you as My own. I covered your blood soaked
wounded flesh with robes of righteousness and
crowns of glory. You feasted upon words from My
very own mouth; words sweeter than honey and good
for the soul. I covered your head with oil. Yes, I
anointed you. I set you before the nations, and now
you have forgotten the Lord your God. Your beauty
and arrogance is as an idol in your own heart. You no
longer worship Me, you desire to be worshipped. You
have become your own god. You now sacrifice the
words I have given you for your beauty and your
pride. The words I fed you are no longer sweet but
bitter to taste in your sight. Your insolence has caused
My flock to fail. You blaspheme the name of the Lord
with your rotten words that sorely vex the bones of
all those who receive them. You sacrificed the
ministry I gave to you and now you sacrifice My
sheep. You are offering up those whom you have no
rights to. You have forgotten your Lord, your
Protector, your Righteousness. You have converted
your beauty into ashes. Because you have forgotten
who you are, your beauty is as dung in My sight. Your

robes will be torn and your shame exposed. Turn from your wicked ways; hear the word of the Lord this day. Turn and live." *May 15, 2009*

3

THE INFLUENCE *of* BABYLON

Cush became the father of Nimrod; he was
the first to be a mighty man on the earth. He
was a mighty hunter before the Lord;
therefore it is said, Like Nimrod, a mighty
hunter before the Lord. The beginning of his
kingdom was Babel, Erech, Accad, and
Calneh, in the land of Shinar [in Babylonia].

—GENESIS 10:8–10

A PERHAPS WELL-KNOWN, but often misused
and underestimated story of the Bible centers
around the tower of Babel and a Nimrod,
literally. Many have become accustomed to
applying "nimrod" to a person who is regarded as
silly, foolish, or stupid. In fact, the way that *nimrod* is
frivolously used, one can falsely assume that the
Nimrod of the Bible was a harmless buffoon with
mediocre plans of building a tower to heaven. On the
contrary, the Word of God reveals an entirely
different story and an entirely different Nimrod.

Further research indicates that what Nimrod
instituted was no meaningless task of a fool, but a
plot to rule the world. Only two verses in the Word

of God speak of him, but they give great insight as to who he was as a person. A distinction was made between Nimrod and all the others before and after him. He was described as a "might hunter" before the Lord," which is often mistranslated and can falsely lead one to believe that Nimrod was once a man of God. However, only two people in the Bible are identified as "hunters," Nimrod and Esau, the twin brother of Jacob. Scripture says, "God loved Jacob, but Esau, He hated" (Rom. 9:13). Thus, the word *hunter* has negative connotations. Also, "before" as used above is *liph'ney* in Hebrew which literally means "to the face of." The verse can be translated as "he made a profaning by being a mighty one in the land." The verse is better translated as "a mighty hunter in place of the Lord" or "mighty hunter against the Lord," implying that Nimrod attempted to stand in the place of God.

It would seem that Nimrod had serious strongholds of pride. He considered himself to be the "mighty hunter," the one who could take God's place. He stood in the face of God and challenged Him in pure, unadulterated rebellion. While it is true that Nimrod was foolish to believe he could replace an almighty God, it is also true that he was a systematic mastermind. Babel marked the beginning of his diabolical, satanic initiative. Genesis 11:1–4 says:

> And the whole earth was of one language and of one accent and mode of expression. And as they journeyed eastward, they found a plain (valley) in the land of Shinar, and they settled and dwelt there. And they said one to another, Come, let us make bricks and burn them thoroughly. So they had brick for stone, and slime (bitumen) for mortar. And they said,

> Come, let us build us a city and a tower whose top reaches into the sky, and let us make a name for ourselves, lest we be scattered over the whole earth.

Nimrod wanted to "make a name" for himself and to become deified. Ironically, Nimrod's feat to reach heaven was not an effort to get closer to God, but further away from Him. Nimrod and the people of Cush's motivation for constructing the tower was rooted in arrogance and selfish ambition. Digging deeper into Nimrod's name, we find that it comes from the Semitic root MRD (marad), meaning "to be rebellious, rebel, and revolt." With rebellion in his heart, his aim was to revolt against God to attain His glory and a high position in the heavens. The tower constructed was called a *ziggurat*, which means "mountaintop or pinnacle." Nimrod's aim was to reach the pinnacle or mountaintop, to become high and lifted up. Some scholars believe that the top of the tower would be dedicated to the heavens upon which they would draw zodiac signs to worship. It is believed to be where astrology and the worship of the elements were instituted[10].

Just as Adam and Eve were falsely promised by the Enemy that they would have God's knowledge and become gods themselves, so was Nimrod. Heavily influenced by Satan, he had dreams of ascending into greater knowledge than God. Nimrod and the people of Cush further rebelled against God in that they did not want to be "scattered abroad." They desired a one humanity, one language tyrannical government that was in rebellion against God's command in Genesis 9:1 to "multiply and fill the earth." Genesis 11:5–9 continues:

> And the Lord came down to see the city and the tower which the sons of men had built. And the Lord said, Behold, they are one people and they have all one language; and this is only the beginning of what they will do, and now nothing they have imagined they can do will be impossible for them. Come, let Us go down and there confound (mix up, confuse) their language, that they may not understand one another's speech. So the Lord scattered them abroad from that place upon the face of the whole earth, and they gave up building the city. Therefore the name of it was called Babel--because there the Lord confounded the language of all the earth; and from that place the Lord scattered them abroad upon the face of the whole earth.

God looked down and saw the people of Cush in direct opposition to His plan and intervened. He knew they had become so influenced by the enemy that they felt indispensable and immortal. The word *imagined* used above is from the Hebrew word *zamam*.[11] It is a primitive root meaning "to plan, usually in a bad sense meaning to devise, plot, and think evil." The imagination is powerful in that it has the potential to produce whatever is imagined. This is why we are instructed in the Word of God to cast down vain imaginations and the high things that exalt themselves against the knowledge of God. (See 2 Corinthians10:5.)

The tower of Babel was no spur of the moment, ludicrous idea of making a tower to reach the heavens just for the mere sake of reaching the heavens. Satan had taken Nimrod and the people of Cush to the top of the mountain, the ziggurat, and offered them the world. Sound familiar? In Matthew 4, Satan took Jesus to the mountain top and offered Him all the kingdoms of the world on the condition that Jesus would fall down and worship him. Though Satan's actions seem presumptuous, it is true that Adam and Eve relinquished the world by their disobedience and Satan is now the ruler of the world systems. (See John 12:31.) Ephesians 6:12 says that the demons are the world rulers (*kosmoskraters*) of darkness. When I use the word *world*, I am speaking of the physical inhabited world, the "cosmos," which is comprised of systems or spheres. The world systems include political, economic, entertainment, education, military, science, technology, and above all, the sphere of religion. The world hates Jesus because He testifies that its works are evil. He is against the very things that the world loves.

In turn, Satan uses the systems of the world to take the minds of the multitudes hostage. "For the god of this world has blinded the unbelievers' minds [that they should not discern the truth], preventing them from seeing the illuminating light of the Gospel of the glory of Christ (the Messiah), who is the Image and Likeness of God" (2 Cor. 4:4). The education system expelled Jesus and prayer from classrooms nationwide. Instead, they promote textbooks that blaspheme about the "Big Bang Theory." The education system is where foundational principles are instilled into youth. When lies are implanted into impressionable minds at an early age, they have the potential to lead them away from God and into the arms of deception.

In this season, Satan is utilizing the entertainment system to promote what God abhors. On any given day, the promotion of premarital sex, homosexual relationships, fornication, and violence can be viewed.

Behaviors that once made us cringe as a nation are now considered normal. Surprisingly, I hear professing Christians say that it is acceptable to open themselves up to various types of songs, movies, and television programs when Satan is "the prince of the power of the air." (See Ephesians 2:2). We live in a time where degrading music and smut-filled entertainment is viewed as harmless or "mere words" when it was upon words that God created the universe. And now Babylon has spilled over into the church in that we have begun to crave lies and entertainment, even from the pulpit.

Apart from the entertainment sphere and the educational sphere, the false religious sphere of Babylon or Babel instituted by Nimrod is the most atrocious of them all. Babylon is responsible for birthing the "great harlot" the false religion system discussed in Revelation 17:1-6.

> One of the seven angels who had the seven bowls then came and spoke to me, saying, Come with me! I will show you the doom (sentence, judgment) of the great harlot (idolatress) who is seated on many waters, [She] with whom the rulers of the earth have joined in prostitution (idolatry) and with the wine of whose immorality (idolatry) the inhabitants of the earth have become intoxicated. And [the angel] bore me away [rapt] in the Spirit into a desert (wilderness), and I saw a woman seated on a scarlet beast that was all covered with blasphemous titles (names), and he had seven heads and ten horns. The woman was robed in purple and scarlet and bedecked with gold, precious stones, and pearls, [and she was] holding in her hand a golden cup full of the accursed offenses and the filth of her lewdness and

vice. And on her forehead there was inscribed a name of mystery [with a secret symbolic meaning]: Babylon the great, the mother of prostitutes (idolatresses) and of the filth and atrocities and abominations of the earth. I also saw that the woman was drunk, [drunk] with the blood of the saints (God's people) and the blood of the martyrs [who witnessed] for Jesus. And when I saw her, I was utterly amazed and wondered greatly.

Babel was a scheme devised to introduce idolatry to the people of God and institute a one world, one religion system of lies. Babel (or Babylon), the instigator of modern paganism, became the mother and source of all pagan religions of the world. Babylon comes from the Hebrew word "Bab-el," which means "confusion." It is also said to be the Hebrew form of the Assyrian word *Bab-ili*, which means "gate of gods." Babylon is responsible for the confusion and the mixing of Paganism, Judaism, and Christianity. It is the hub for New Age beliefs, Scientology, Buddhism, Islamism, and a host of other false doctrine.

Ancient records indicate that Nimrod did not act alone in his initiative. In fact, it is said that he had a wife named Semiramis whose influence was even greater than his. She was believed to be the spearhead behind the satanic, pagan movements of false religion. Semiramis, whose name means "highest heaven," was believed to be the founder and first high priestess of the Babylonian mystery religion, a system of apostasy. It is said that the initiation into the mystery religion included a mystery drink of honey, wine flour, and water, which represented the doctrines of the cult[12].

Why a drink of wine, flour, honey, and water? Let's examine what Numbers 15:9–10 says:

> Then shall one offer with the bull a cereal offering of three tenths of an ephah of fine flour mixed with half a hin of oil. And you shall bring for the drink offering half a hin of wine for an offering made by fire, of a pleasant and soothing fragrance to the Lord.

Leviticus 2:11 says:

> No cereal offering that you bring to the Lord shall be made with leaven, for you shall burn no leaven or honey in any offering made by fire to the Lord.

Flour and wine sufficed as acceptable sacrifices to the Lord. However, no sacrifice was ever to be mixed with honey. When yeast and honey are mixed together, the yeast feeds on the honey and gives off a gas, called carbon dioxide. The honey is symbolic of sugarcoated doctrines that are spreading across the world giving carbon dioxide (breath) to the false religious system. In this hour, we have begun to taint sacrifice unto God with our own ideas. The mystery drink or doctrine centers on perverting true worship of God. Proverbs 5:3-5 says:

> For the lips of a loose woman drip honey as a honeycomb, and her mouth is smoother than oil; But in the end she is bitter as wormwood, sharp as a two-edged and devouring sword. Her feet go down to death; her steps take hold of Sheol (Hades, the place of the dead).

While the adulteress is often pretty to look at and perhaps exciting to be with, the end is pain and her destination is Sheol. The false doctrine of Babylon has caused many to become intoxicated upon sugarcoated, watered- down lies. To the multitudes, it's appealing and seemingly easy, but it all has the same ending—hell. As believers, our bellies should be filled only with the Word of God. His Word is life and is already sweeter than honey. (See Ezekiel 3:3.) There is no need to add man-made sugar substitutes.

Semiramis was also known as "Astarte or Ashtoreth," whom the children of Israel were guilty of worshiping. *Astarte* means "the woman who made towers," which indicates that Semiramis continued to build upon the false religious system even after Nimrods' death. The children of Israel forsook God for the false goddess Ashtoreth in the following verses:

> And they forsook the Lord and served Baal
> [the god worshiped by the Canaanites] and the
> Ashtaroth [female deities such as Ashtoreth
> and Asherah].
>
> —JUDGES 2:13

> Because they have forsaken Me and have
> worshiped Ashtoreth the goddess of the
> Sidonians, Chemosh the god of the Moabites,
> and Milcom the god of the Ammonites, and
> have not walked in My ways, to do what is
> right in My sight, keeping My statutes and My
> ordinances as did David his father.
>
> —1 KINGS 11:33

> And the king defiled the high places east of
> Jerusalem, south of the Mount of Corruption,
> which Solomon the king of Israel had built for
> Ashtoreth the abominable [goddess] of the
> Sidonians, for Chemosh the abominable god
>
> of the Moabites, and for Milcom the
> abominable [god] of the Ammonites.
>
> —2 KINGS 23:13

It is said that after Nimrod died, Semiramis proclaimed him as the sun god, Baal. She even went as far as to declare that she was visited by a spirit of Nimrod and supernaturally conceived. Later she would "miraculously" give birth to a child, Tammuz who was also said to be Nimrod reincarnated. Her son is said to have been killed by a wild beast and then brought back to life. She blasphemed that he was the Savior, the Seed promised in Genesis 3:15. This was deception from the Enemy so that the true Seed, Jesus Christ, would not be recognized when He came into the world. The religious system of worship by Semiramis and Tammuz involved male and female prostitution, sexual orgies, homosexuality, bestiality, unnatural sacrifices, fornication, intoxication and all other forms of lewdness and immorality. Ezekiel 8:13–14 speaks of Tammuz, which says:

> He also said to me, Yet again you shall see greater abominations which they are committing. Then He brought me to the entrance of the north gate of the Lord's house; and behold, there sat women weeping for Tammuz [a Babylonian god, who was supposed to die annually and subsequently be resurrected].

The Babylonian religion is called a "mystery religion" because many are "too intelligent" to worship Satan directly. So the Enemy creates mysteries or false religions that don't profess the worship of Satan but neither do they include true worship of God. Satan mixes Christianity with lies to further confuse the world, many times even the elect.

Babylon influences believers across the globe to choose immorality and become intoxicated upon falsehood and sin, causing them to incorporate doctrines of demons into their messages. A spirit of Nimrod is visiting many leaders nowadays and they are giving birth to deception. If, in fact, leaders are guilty of this, then they are no better than New Age believers or scientologists, because any doctrine taught in portion is false doctrine. Any world religion or alleged truth that is not the Word of God has descended from Babylon and has ascended to a place in the heart where only God should reign.

Looking once more at the Semitic root of Nimrod's name, M-R-D, we see that it is the origin of the word *MaRauDer* or *MuRDer*. To murder is "to put an end to" or "to destroy." The Babylonian influence seeks to destroy the truth. It is gaining more and more ammunition, targeting the saints of God for the sole purpose of killing truth, stealing souls, and destroying lives with lies.

I dreamed of an elderly, white bearded prophet, clothed in tattered rags upon a rocking ship. In his hands was a Bible that he grasped closely to his heart as the boat swayed from side to side upon boisterous waves. Now with the Bible clutched firmly in his hands, he lifted it toward the heavens. Speaking loudly and passionately, he exclaimed, "This is not only scripture; it is truth." Near him was a man who dropped his Bible repeatedly, only recovering certain pages and leaving some on the floor. In other parts of the ship, were other "saints" who, behind closed doors, indulged in every abominable act known to man.

The ship represents ministries across the nation being tossed back and forth upon waves of unsound doctrine. The prophet standing in the midst of the boat represents the Word of God being spoken uncompromisingly in a world engaging in lust, passion, and the desires of the flesh.

I heard the Lord say, "There are many seeking their own scent and not the fragrance of Christ. Like a dog that chases its tail, many are going in circles seeking and looking in all the wrong places, trying to fill a space that their carnal desires cannot fill because only I can. They're lukewarm, losing themselves in sin. They're not who I created them to be, picking up the gospel and putting it back down again, not holding on to what is necessary to sustain them; putting too much emphasis on how they live materialistically and not who they are living for; searching, never finding, and seeking with closed eyes; hearers only and not doers; picking and choosing which part of the gospel they wish to believe; perverting the gospel to suit their perverse needs and carnality. One thing stands, the Word of God, the Holy Scripture. Let everything and everyone who perverts or denies the full gospel be a lie, but the Word of God be truth, forever and always." *May 31, 2009*

The word *scripture* can be defined as "the sacred writing of any religion or anything that is written." Therefore, it is important to remember that the Word of God is not only Scripture; it is the absolute Truth. Demons have developed false scripture over the years, but there remains only one Truth. The Word of God explicitly warns that the church age will be characterized by growing apostasy. Second Timothy 3:13 says:

> But wicked men and imposters will go on
> from bad to worse, deceiving *and* leading

astray others and being deceived *and* led astray themselves.

Second Peter 2:1-3 says:

> But also [in those days] there arose false prophets among the people, just as there will be false teachers among yourselves, who will subtly and stealthily introduce heretical doctrines (destructive heresies), even denying and disowning the Master Who bought them, bringing upon themselves swift destruction. And many will follow their immoral ways and lascivious doings; because of them the true Way will be maligned and defamed. And in their covetousness (lust, greed) they will exploit you with false (cunning) arguments. From of old the sentence [of condemnation] for them has not been idle; their destruction (eternal misery) has not been asleep.

The influence of Babylon is causing many to fall away from what it means to be true Christians. True Christians understand that Word of God is not merely scripture that can be altered to make people comfortable in the midst of their sin.

In another dream, I saw a small house once owned by a married couple. The husband left his wife for another woman, his mistress. Merely a few feet away from the humble home the couple once shared, the adulterous husband built a huge new house for his mistress. It was monstrous in height and was shaped like a temple as it had a huge cross on top of it. The house was built very quickly, the same day that he left his wife. On the top floor in one of the bedrooms the mistress waited for the adulterous husband. She was so filled with lust that she could hardly wait for him to fulfill them. Ezekiel 16:30-31 reads:

> How weak and spent with longing and lust is your heart and mind, says the Lord God, seeing you do all these things, the work of a bold, domineering harlot, In that you build your vaulted place (brothel) at the head of every street and make your high place at every crossing. But you were not like a harlot because you scorned pay.

Many unfaithful members of the body of Christ have been seduced away. Like Nimrod, they have built lives for themselves based upon greed, lust, and lies. They unknowingly form their own churches (religions) almost overnight based upon carnality while attempting to tear down the house of God. The Babylonian influence of this world is one that seductively whispers "Make a name for yourself." Sadly many leaders are following that voice instead of the voice of the Almighty. First Corinthians 3:10-15 says:

> According to the grace (the special endowment for my task) of God bestowed on me, like a skillful architect and master builder I laid [the] foundation, and now another [man] is building upon it. But let each [man] be careful how he builds upon it, For no other foundation can anyone lay than that which is[already] laid, which is Jesus Christ (the Messiah, the Anointed One). But if anyone builds upon the Foundation, whether it be with gold, silver, precious stones, wood, hay, straw, The work of each [one] will become [plainly, openly] known (shown for what it is); for the day [of Christ] will disclose and declare it, because it will be revealed with fire, and the fire will test and critically appraise the character and worth of the work each person has done. If the work which any person has built on this Foundation [any product of his efforts whatever] survives [this test], he will

> get his reward. But if any person's work is burned up [under the test], he will suffer the loss [of it all, losing his reward], though he himself will be saved, but only as [one who has passed] through fire.

Even though these so-called "truths" are erected across the world, there is but one that is everlasting— the inerrant Word of God, the whole Truth. John 2:19-22 says:

> Jesus answered them, Destroy (undo) this temple, and in three days I will raise it up again. Then the Jews replied, It took forty-six years to build this temple (sanctuary), and will You raise it up in three days? But He had spoken of the temple which was His body. When therefore He had risen from the dead, His disciples remembered that He said this. And so they believed and trusted and relied on the Scripture and the word (message) Jesus had spoken.

Genesis 10:10 says that Babylon began, and Revelation indicates that it will end. (See Revelation 18:2 and Revelation 20:10.) However, there is no end to the kingdom of God, His Word endures forever.

4

THE SPIRIT *of* JEZEBEL

> But I have this against you: that you tolerate
> the woman Jezebel, who calls herself a
> prophetess [claiming to be inspired], and who
> is teaching and leading astray my servants and
> beguiling them into practicing sexual vice and
> eating food sacrificed to idols.
>
> —REVELATION 2:20

JEZEBEL IS A name that has taken on many connotations over the years. In fact, almost too often, the term is applied to a sexually seductive woman. She's cohabitates with men, caring nothing about entering into the covenant of marriage. She's the sexual vixen who is not to be trusted around husbands. She is the harlot, a loose woman, with the seductive ability to use what she has to get exactly what she wants. Even the dictionary defines *jezebel* as a "shameless impudent and scheming woman."

While many have taken this word and used it rather loosely to describe a woman who dresses provocatively and steals husbands, the truth is that Queen Jezebel most likely dressed herself in what she considered to be "priestly" garments of Baal. Much

99

like Christians, her garments represented who she was inside. But instead of wearing robes of righteousness, she was clothed in wickedness. So with that myth dispelled, we see that her seductiveness had nothing to do with her outward attire. This is a common misconception because even in the church today, many misjudge others based upon outward appearance alone. Harlotry is not only about miniskirts worn on a body; we should be more concerned about those who are clothed in white, but wear miniskirts upon their hearts.

We must not underestimate and misjudge Jezebel, reducing her to a scheming sexual temptress who merely focused on ensnaring men. Harlotry was not only what she did, it embodied who she was. Seductiveness was at her core. While Jezebel of the Bible was highly seductive in nature, her scheming aimed much further than the home of a married couple. The plot of Jezebel was far deeper; she desired to seduce the nation into idolatry.

UNHOLY ALLIANCE

In the thirty-eighth year of Asa king of Judah, Ahab son of Omri began his reign of twenty-two years over Israel in Samaria. And Ahab son of Omri did evil in the sight of the Lord above all before him. As if it had been a light thing for Ahab to walk in the sins of Jeroboam son of Nebat, he took for a wife Jezebel daughter of Ethbaal king of the Sidonians, and served Baal and worshiped him. He erected an altar for Baal in the house of Baal which he built in Samaria. And Ahab made an Asherah [idolatrous symbol of the goddess Asherah]. Ahab did more to provoke

the Lord, the God of Israel, to anger than all
the kings of Israel before him.

—1 KINGS 16:29–33

Jezebel's father was Ethbaal, which means
"one who rules with Baal" or "together with
Baal." His name alone testified to whom he was
devoted and denotes a deeper tie into the false
demonic world of Baalam. Ethbaal was a high priest
of Baal, meaning he was more than a mere worshiper
of Baal; he was spiritually united with him. Thus it is
easy to understand why Jezebel was highly
enthusiastic about and devoted to Balaam. Her father
was married to him and she was the seed of Satan.
She grew up desiring nothing more than to do his
will. (See John 8:44.)

When Ahab married Jezebel, he changed alliances.
An alliance is "a situation when two seeming political
antagonists temporarily join together in order to fight
a common political enemy." It becomes unholy when
lines are crossed and morals are compromised, which
was the case with King Ahab. No longer serving God,
he promoted Baal, leaving the gate open. Baal means
various things throughout the Bible, usually "master"
or "owner," but it also means "lord of the flies." The
unholy alliance between Jezebel and Ahab was
responsible for allowing "flies" or "doctrines of Baal"
to seep into the house of God, provoking Him to
anger.

The marriage between Jezebel and Ahab was not
only a spiritual alliance, but also a political alliance.
Their union provided both sides with military
protection from powerful enemies as well as valuable
trade routes. Israel gained access to the Phoenician
ports; Phoenicia gained passage through Israel's

central hill. It is evident from the beginning that Ahab and Jezebel's marriage was not one rooted in love, but in greed.

The name Jezebel, Phoenician in origin, means "un-husbanded." Although she married Ahab, her lack of submission and hunger for control, proved that marriage was just another word. Needless to say, Jezebel was not your typical bride. In her eyes, marriage was nothing more than a business arrangement and a platform. She submitted to no one and instead demanded Ahab to submit to her. Not only did Ahab and Jezebel's marriage allow her to become queen, but it also allowed her to take the place of King Ahab, usurping his authority.

In this hour, many unholy alliances are being orchestrated between the world and the church. We are commanded, "Do not be conformed to this world (this age), [fashioned after and adapted to its external, superficial customs]" (Rom. 12:2). The New Living Translation says, "Don't copy the behavior and customs of this world." We should not look like, act like, or smell like the world. But we are imitating them, looking like them, and sadly borrowing from them. However, we must begin to make our allegiance sure. We must choose whose side we are on, God's or the world's.

AHAB AND JEZEBEL COLLABORATION

> Now Naboth the Jezreelite had a vineyard in Jezreel, close beside the palace of Ahab king of Samaria; and after these things, Ahab said to Naboth, Give me your vineyard, that I may have it for a garden of herbs, because it is near my house. I will give you a better vineyard for it or, if you prefer, I will give you its worth in

102

money. Naboth said to Ahab, The Lord forbid that I should give the inheritance of my fathers to you. And Ahab [already depressed by the Lord's message to him] came into his house [more] resentful and sullen because of what Naboth the Jezreelite had said to him; for he had said, I will not give you the inheritance of my fathers. And he lay down on his bed, turned away his face, and would eat no food.... Jezebel his wife said to him, Do you not govern Israel? Arise, eat food, and let your heart be happy. I will give you the vineyard of Naboth the Jezreelite. So she wrote letters in Ahab's name and sealed them with his seal and sent them to the elders and nobles who dwelt with Naboth in his city.

—1 KINGS 21:1–4, 7, 8

While the spirit of Jezebel is often discussed independently, the spirit of Jezebel and the spirit of Ahab clearly function together. Jezebel's agent of harlotry was her very own husband, King Ahab. Wherever the spirit of Jezebel is allowed to dominate, you will find a spirit of Ahab, marked by intimidation. In the text above, we see that Ahab was greedy; he coveted land that rightly belonged to Naboth. After Naboth stood his ground and refused, Ahab went home and sulked until his bride asked, "What's wrong with you? Why are you not eating?" Paraphrasing, he replied, "Because I can't get what belongs to someone else." Jezebel stroked his ego, saying, "Are you not king?" and "I'll get what belongs to someone else for you." She took pride and pleasure in tearing down the people of God for the sake of gain, but even more than gain, she craved power.

Likewise, the spirit of Ahab targets what rightfully belongs to God's people, it seeks to steal the inheritance of the saints. The spirit of Ahab influences one to deny the principles of the Lord for financial wealth and political gain. Ahab was a manipulator just like his bride. He was the instigator of murder, and Jezebel was the murderer. Proverbs 7:21-22 says:

> With much justifying *and* enticing argument she persuades him, with the allurements of her lips she leads him [to overcome his conscience and his fears] *and* forces him along. Suddenly he [yields and] follows her reluctantly like an ox moving to the slaughter, like one in fetters going to the correction [to be given] to a fool *or like a dog enticed by food to the muzzle.*

King Ahab did everything in his power to please his bride. He remained silent as she murdered the innocent; he said nothing as she erected false gods throughout the kingdom. No matter what heinous act Jezebel committed, Ahab, as a husband or king never rebuked her.

We too have entered into a time where there is an absence of correction in the body of Christ. This "people-pleasing" spirit that is running rampant is one that avoids discipline. The spirits of Ahab and Jezebel work collaboratively to compel leaders to compromise by developing lightness toward sin. Those influenced by the spirit of Jezebel dares anyone to correct them, and the spirit of Ahab causes leaders to shy away from issues that need to be corrected. The spirit of Jezebel is carrying out the intimidation while those influenced by spirit of Ahab, submits in fear.

We see this manifested when leaders are afraid to discuss certain topics because of the fear that members will leave their ministry. "Jezebel" sits in the audience threatening to leave with half of the members, and "Ahab" stands behind the pulpit afraid to speak the truth because he desires members or financial stability. Sadly, those affected by this spirit are more concerned with full churches than they are with speaking forth truth in love. The spirit of Ahab is cunning in that its passiveness is a cover for its greed. 1 Kings 21:15–16 says:

> Then Jezebel said to Ahab, Arise, take possession of the vineyard of Naboth the Jezreelite which he refused to sell you, for Naboth is not alive, but dead. When Ahab heard that, he arose to go down to the vineyard of Naboth the Jezreelite to take possession of it.

The spirit of Jezebel operates today exactly as it always has. It manipulates leaders, enticing them with land, property, wealth, and fame. It strokes egos and whispers, "Are you not the king of all the land? Let me do this for you, and let me control this." It is a controlling spirit that hates true leadership and seeks to murder and conspire against them at all costs. If unsuccessful at converting true ministers by ways of manipulation, it seeks vengeance. What it can't control, it attempts to kill.

THE SEED OF JEZEBEL AND AHAB

AHAZIAH

> [King] Ahaziah fell down through a lattice in his upper chamber in Samaria and lay sick. He sent messengers, saying, Go, ask Baal-zebub, the god of [Philistine] Ekron, if I shall recover from this illness. But the angel of the Lord

said to Elijah the Tishbite, Arise, go up to meet the messengers of the king in Samaria and say to them, Is it because there is no God in Israel that you are going to inquire of Baal-zebub, the god of Ekron? Therefore the Lord says: You [Ahaziah] shall not leave the bed on which you lie, but shall surely die. And Elijah departed. When the messengers returned to Ahaziah, he said, Why have you turned back? They replied, A man came up to meet us who said, Go back to the king who sent you and tell him, Thus says the Lord: Is there no God in Israel that you send to inquire of Baal-zebub, the god of Ekron? Therefore you shall not leave the bed on which you lie, but shall surely die. The king asked, What was the man like who came to meet you saying these things? They answered, He was a hairy man with a girdle of leather about his loins. And he said, It is Elijah the Tishbite. Then the king sent to Elijah a captain of fifty men with his fifty [to seize him]. He found Elijah sitting on a hilltop and said, Man of God, the king says: Come down.

—2 KINGS 1:2–9

Ahaziah was king after the death of his father Ahab. He "did evil in the sight of the Lord, and walked in the ways of his father and his mother." (See 1 Kings 22:52.) Verse 2 says that Ahaziah fell through the lattice of his upper room in Samaria. The word *lattice* means "an opening or a window," but can also be defined as an "organization or a system." Proverbs 7:4-7 says:

Say to skillful *and* godly Wisdom, You are my sister, and regard understanding *or* insight as your intimate friend—That they may keep you from the loose woman, from the adventuress who flatters with *and* makes smooth her

106

words. For at the window of my house I looked out through my lattice. And among the simple (empty-headed and empty-hearted) ones, I perceived among the youths a young man void of good sense.

Ahab and Jezebel produced empty-headed seed that fell into the world system, also known as Babylon, which is ruled by Satan. Like his parents, he hated the truth and preferred lies. God sent Elijah, the prophet, with a true word, but Ahaziah refused to listen and responded by attempting to murder the messenger of truth. Instead of repenting and turning to God, he turned to the enemy, Baal-zebub—the lord of the flies—for answers. The wisdom of God is much needed in the hour to break the back of harlotry in our nation.

We live in a generation where many are falling into the Babylonian system of false religion and doctrine. After opening themselves up to lies for so long, many no longer discern the voice of God. So when God sends them a true word through His minister, the individual cannot recognize it and becomes enraged. In their fallen state, instead of looking up to the Lord, they continue to practice unholy lifestyles and look for leaders to give them false words of compromise. Their desire is a word that does not rebuke them, but one that comforts them in the midst of their wrongdoing. I have witnessed leaders locally and nationally who have been found in known sin. But what shocked me the most is the nonchalant attitude and lightness towards the things God hates. Instead of spiritual parents rebuking the fallen in hopes that they'd be healed, they barely received a slap on the wrist and were prematurely placed back upon platforms as though no offense occurred. Many of the "spiritual parents" use the excuse "who am I to judge" and turn away from the sinful behavior of their seed. However, there is a difference between judgment and holy rebuke. Many support lewd behavior, because it comforts them in their own lewdness. Even in a fallen state where death is promised, many still turn their ears to voices of heresy rather than the voice of truth. This is evident throughout the Word of God.

> Woe to you, scribes and Pharisees, pretenders (hypocrites)! For you build tombs for the prophets and decorate the monuments of the righteous, Saying, If we had lived in the days of our forefathers, we would not have aided them in shedding the blood of the prophets. Thus you are testifying against yourselves that you are the descendants of those who murdered the prophets.
>
> —MATTHEW 23:29–31

JORAM

> Joram son of Ahab became king of Israel in Samaria in the eighteenth year of Jehoshaphat king of Judah, and he reigned twelve years. He did evil in the eyes of the Lord, but not as his father and mother had done. He got rid of the sacred stone of Baal that his father had made. Nevertheless he clung to the sins of Jeroboam son of Nebat, which he had caused Israel to commit; he did not turn away from them.
>
> —2 KINGS 3:1–3

Joram became king after the accidental death of his brother, Ahaziah. The Bible characterizes him as evil because during his twelve-year reign, he continuously wavered back and forth. In fact, because of Joram's sin, his time as king was plagued with multiple multi-year famines. These were wake-up calls from God to which Joram never responded. One moment he was cordial with Elisha; the next he persecuted him. There were times when he was faithful to the Lord; other times he blamed Him for problems caused by his own sin. He took steps against the Baal worship introduced by his father, but observed false idols. He was lukewarm and thus good for nothing. Time after time, God displayed His awesome power by rescuing Joram in many great miracles worked by the prophet. Yet, despite evidence, he never trusted Him.

We live in a world where there is a constant back and forth wavering between loyalties. The world is in one of the worst economic crisis it has been in, in quite some time, which is a direct result of our indifference toward God as a nation. It is time to wake up because "the one who wavers (hesitates, doubts) is like the billowing surge out at sea that is blown hither and thither and tossed by the wind. For truly, let not such a person imagine that he will receive anything [he asks for] from the Lord, [For being as he is] a man of two minds (hesitating, dubious, irresolute), [he is] unstable and unreliable and uncertain about everything [he thinks, feels, decides]" (Jas 1:6-8).

ATHALIAH

> When Athaliah the mother of [King] Ahaziah [of Judah] saw that her son was dead, she arose and destroyed all the royal descendants. But Jehosheba, the daughter of King Jehoram, [half] sister of Ahaziah, stole Joash son of Ahaziah from among the king's sons, who

were to be slain, even him and his nurse, and
hid them from Athaliah in an inner storeroom
for beds; so he was not slain. Joash was with
his nurse hidden in the house of the Lord for
six years. And Athaliah reigned over the land.

—2 KINGS 11:1–3

Athaliah, Queen of Judah from 842–836 B.C., was
just as evil as her parents, Ahab and Jezebel. In fact,
she was guilty of killing all the members of the royal
family who were seen as threats to her obtaining the
throne. All except Joash, whose name means "fire of
God." Athaliah was able to slay all but one of her
grandchildren; she could not put out the fire of God.
Many self-professing spiritual parents are guilty of
slaying the children of God with falsehood.
Their harlotrous nature infects those around them,
attempting to extinguish the fire of God in the bellies
of true ministers, but it is impossible.

In a dream, I saw a male prostitute who was
involved in an unholy relationship with a woman.
This relationship continued without fail until one day
a true leader of God showed up at the door of the
hotel room where the illicit affair took place.
Convicted, the male prostitute began to explain to the
woman that he could no longer engage in the
inappropriate relationship with her. As he was leaving,
the woman, lying in the bed, threatened to kill the
both of them. She further boasted, "I've chopped off
the feet of many men," insinuating that he would be
next. After hearing this, the man became frightened
for his life; he ran a great distance and hid inside of a
box, just in case the woman came to look for him.
She never did.

The spirit of Jezebel is responsible for chopping off the feet of many men and women of God; it specializes in hindering their walk. So we as the body of Christ can no longer afford to sleep with the Enemy. Unholy alliances must be severed no matter the cost. Proverbs 7:25-27 says:

> Let not your heart incline toward her ways, do not stray into her paths. For she has cast down many wounded; indeed, all her slain are a mighty host. Her house is the way to Sheol (Hades, the place of the dead), going down to the chambers of death.

The spirit of Jezebel operates heavily in intimidation causing the mighty to run and hide. Just ask Elijah. But we must remember "greater is He that is in us than he that is in the world" (1 John 4:4). The spirit of Jezebel boasts of killing the truth, but we as Christians boast of Him who is the Truth. (See John 14:6.)

5

THE SPIRIT *of* BELIAL

> Do not be unequally yoked with unbelievers
> [do not make mismated alliances with them or
> come under a different yoke with them,
> inconsistent with your faith]. For what
> partnership have right living and right
> standing with God with iniquity and
> lawlessness? Or how can light have fellowship
> with darkness? What harmony can there be
> between Christ and Belial [the devil]? Or what
> has a believer in common with an unbeliever?
>
> —2 CORINTHIANS 6:14–15

UNLIKE THE OTHER spirits discussed thus far, Belial is not a biblical name given to a specific person of the Bible. Instead, it is shown in phrases such as "sons of Belial" and is used to describe many unnamed people. The term Belial is of Hebrew origin and means "worthless."

> A worthless man devises and digs up mischief,
> and in his lips there is as a scorching fire.
>
> —PROVERBS16:27

> A worthless person, a wicked man, is he who goes about with a perverse (contrary, wayward) mouth.

—PROVERBS 6:12

The word *worthless*[13] is defined as "unworthy," "lacking in value or merit," and "morally reprehensible." It further describes a person that is vile, slimy, and ugly in their actions. This is a person with "evil purpose, an evil influence, and evil deeds." The spirit of Belial is alive and in operation in the world today. In order to understand the dismantling of this spirit, we must first understand how it functions.

1. SEDUCES AWAY FROM THE TRUTH

> Certain men, the children of Belial, are gone out from among you, and have withdrawn the inhabitants of their city, saying, Let us go and serve other gods, which ye have not known; then shalt thou enquire, and make search, and ask diligently; and, behold, if it be truth, and the thing certain, that such abomination is wrought among you.

—DEUTERONOMY 13:13–14, KJV

The spirit of Belial targets God's ministers and leadership (especially with the temptation of sexual sin). The Amplified version of verse 13 says the children of Belial, "entices them away." The term *entice* is defined as "to provoke someone to do something through (often false or exaggerated) promises or persuasion." The worthless spirit of Belial functions as a master of seduction, enticing individuals away with false promises and false hopes. It causes one to commit apostasy and abandon loyalty, changing alliances for the hope of something "better." This spirit seduces believers away from the truth and into the doctrines of demons. "The [Holy] Spirit distinctly and expressly declares that in latter times some will turn away from the faith, giving attention to deluding and seducing spirits and doctrines that demons teach, through the hypocrisy and pretensions of liars whose consciences are seared (cauterized)" (1 Tim. 4:1).

2. SEARS THE CONSCIENCE

When Gentiles who have not the [divine] Law do instinctively what the Law requires, they are a law to themselves, since they do not have the Law. They show that the essential requirements of the Law are written in their hearts and are operating there, with which their consciences (sense of right and wrong) also bear witness; and their [moral] decisions (their arguments of reason, their condemning or approving thoughts) will accuse or perhaps defend and excuse [them].

—ROMANS 2:14–15

God has placed basic principles of His Law in every person's conscience, regardless of whether or not a person ever reads the Bible or has been told anything about Him. The conscience is defined as "an inherited moral and ethical knowledge and awareness that intellectually and emotionally guides us in differing between good and evil." Our conscience was given after the fall of Adam and Eve in the Garden of

Eden. Before then, there was no need of a conscience because there was no knowledge of good and evil.

The word *sear* means "withered and dried up." The spirit of Belial causes one's conscience, the moral and ethical check system to become withered and dried up. This happens when the conscience is constantly ignored. Like most, when I read of horrendous acts taking place in the world, I find myself wondering how a person could be so evil. How could someone commit adultery after fifty years of being devoted to that person? How could a mother murder her very own child? How could a human being fly an airplane into a building, killing thousands of innocent people? It's because their conscience has been completely destroyed and their heart no longer has a check-and-balance mechanism to instruct them otherwise. Without a conscience, all manner of evil is devised in hearts and evil deeds are committed without true repentance or looking back. Belial is the culprit behind perversion and is the driving force behind rape, murder, homosexuality, and perversion the gospel.

3. LACKS REVERENCE FOR GOD

Now the sons of Eli were sons of Belial; they knew not the LORD. And the priest's custom with the people was, that, when any man offered sacrifice, the priest's servant came, while the flesh was in seething, with a fleshhook of three teeth in his hand; And he struck it into the pan, or kettle, or caldron, or pot; all that the fleshhook brought up the priest took for himself. So they did in Shiloh unto all the Israelites that came thither.

—1 SAMUEL 2:12–14, KJV

Isaiah 5 speaks of God and His *vineyard*, which was representative of His people, Israel. While planting His vineyard, He expected grapes but instead His vineyard yielded wild grapes. The word *wild* is from the Hebrew word, *beushim* which means "worthless and stinking things." Eli was a direct descendant of Aaron, (the first high priest); he, his sons, and their descendants would have continued to be inheritors of the priesthood forever. (See Exodus 29:9.) So although Eli's sons, Hophni and Phinehas, were worthless and stinking with corruption, initially they had purpose. God expected more from them but they were putrid "calling evil good and good evil, putting darkness for light and light for darkness and putting bitter for sweet and sweet for bitter!" (See Isaiah 5:20.) The sons of Eli were "sons of Belial" because even though they were raised knowing of God, they did not know Him. And because they did not care to know Him, they forfeited their destinies for the momentary pleasures of the flesh.

> Their doings will not permit them to return to their God, for the spirit of harlotry is within them and they know not the Lord [they do not recognize, appreciate, give heed to, or cherish the Lord].
>
> —HOSEA 5:4

Knowing of God and knowing Him intimately are two entirely different things. The word *know* is used casually today in that someone whom we meet, we automatically claim to know that individual, when the truth is we only have knowledge of the person's existence. To *know* is "to discern the character or nature of." Eli's sons obviously had never had an encounter with God because it takes knowing Him to truly reverence Him.

> The reverent and worshipful fear of the Lord is the beginning (the chief and choice part) of Wisdom, and the knowledge of the Holy One is insight and understanding.

—PROVERBS 9:10

We live in a generation much like Eli's sons, because though many claim to know God, it is evident in their behavior and lifestyle choices that they do not. (See Judges 2:10.) There is no holy reverence because they have not had true experiences with the King of Kings. As a result, it has become second nature for the world and even the saints, to act as though God does not exist at all.

4. DISRESPECTS GOD'S COMMANDS

> Also before they burnt the fat, the priest's servant came, and said to the man that sacrificed, Give flesh to roast for the priest; for he will not have sodden flesh of thee, but raw. And if any man said unto him, Let them not fail to burn the fat presently, and then take as much as thy soul desireth; then he would answer him, Nay; but thou shalt give it me now: and if not, I will take it by force. Wherefore the sin of the young men was very great before the LORD: for men abhorred the offering of the LORD.... And there came a man of God unto Eli, and said unto him, Thus saith the LORD, Did I plainly appear unto the house of thy father, when they were in Egypt in Pharaoh's house? And did I choose him out of all the tribes of Israel to be my priest, to offer upon mine altar, to burn incense, to wear an ephod before me? and did

> I give unto the house of thy father all the
> offerings made by fire of the children of
> Israel? Wherefore kick ye at my sacrifice and
> at mine offering, which I have commanded in
> my habitation; and honourest thy sons above
> me, to make yourselves fat with the chiefest
> of all the offerings of Israel my people?
>
> —1 SAMUEL 2:15–17, 27-29, KJV

Hophni and Phinehas abhorred the offering of God, meaning they dealt contemptuously with it. The fat of the meat sacrifice was considered the best part. God's portion was to be given first; however, Hophni and Phinehas demanded their portion first. Demanding the meat before the sacrifice was a way of robbing God.

The spirit of Belial causes blatant disobedience and disrespect to the Lord. Leaders' intentions have become compromised by this spirit so much so, that all manner of evil occurs within the very walls of the sanctuary with no repercussions. Many in high positions with authority once given to them by God have allowed their hearts to become deceived by the spirit of Belial. They have acted disdainfully with the flock of God. They are irresponsible leaders interested in feeding their own bellies and not feeding His children. "Yes, the dogs are greedy; they never have enough. And such are the shepherds who cannot understand; they have all turned to their own way, each one to his own gain, from every quarter [one and all]" (Isa. 56:11).

5. CAUSES LEADERS TO IGNORE SIN

And the LORD said to Samuel, Behold, I will do a thing in Israel, at which both the ears of

119

every one that heareth it shall tingle. In that day I will perform against Eli all things which I have spoken concerning his house: when I begin, I will also make an end. For I have told him that I will judge his house for ever for the iniquity which he knoweth; because his sons made themselves vile, and he restrained them not. And therefore I have sworn unto the house of Eli, that the iniquity of Eli's house shall not be purged with sacrifice nor offering forever.

—1 SAMUEL 3:11–14, KJV

If I say to the wicked, You shall surely die, and you do not give him warning or speak to warn the wicked to turn from his wicked way, to save his life, the same wicked man shall die in his iniquity, but his blood will I require at your hand.

—EZEKIEL 3:18

The spirit of Belial works by blinding leaders to the sin in their midst. It brings with it the spirits of fear, intimidation, and compromise. It causes a house that was once blessed of the Lord to carry a curse; a house of worth becomes worthless. Leaders around the world are turning their heads to sin and allowing foul spirits to roam freely and wreak havoc in the very house of God.

In a dream set in ancient times, I watched two men both clothed in huge brown mantles walking around inside of a cave. The older man was the spiritual father to the younger one. As they were excavating the cave, they discovered a pit. On the side of the pit was a handle that could be pulled to open it and see what was inside. The father knew that they should not open it. However, the son was curious and insisted that they did. Instead of instructing the young man to keep the pit closed, the leader turned his head and foolishly allowed him to pull the handle. After which, several snakes jumped out, the largest one bit the leader. Proverbs 6:12-15 says:

> A worthless person, a wicked man, Walks with a perverse mouth; He winks with his eyes, He shuffles his feet, He points with his fingers; Perversity *is* in his heart, He devises evil continually, He sows discord. Therefore his calamity shall come suddenly; Suddenly he shall be broken without remedy.

1 Samuel 4 reveals that Hophni and Phinehas lost their lives in the heat of battle with the Philistines. They foolishly assumed that because they had the Ark —symbolic of the Presence of God—with them, that they would be protected even in the midst of their rebellion. Like Nadab and Abihu they put their unclean hands upon what was holy and were suddenly killed as a result. Eli, then 98 years old and blind, heard the news and fell off his seat backward to his death. (See 1 Samuel 4: 15, 18.)

Like the leader in the dream, Eli had every opportunity to rebuke his rebellious sons, however, he refused. He knew of the offenses his sons were committing, but in response to their lewd behavior, he turned a deaf ear. Finally, because of his insolence, judgment found him and the blood of his sons was on his hands. Leaders of God must stand up and properly lead those in their care, because it is they who will be held accountable for their insolence and negligence. We must not be blind, thinking that God will turn the other way while His people are led astray. Judgment will find us no matter who we are.

6. CAUSES BARRENNESS

> Now as they were making their hearts merry, behold, the men of the city, certain sons of Belial, beset the house round about, and beat at the door, and spake to the master of the house, the old man, saying, Bring forth the man that came into thine house, that we may know him….But the men would not hearken to him: so the man took his concubine, and brought her forth unto them; and they knew her, and abused her all the night until the morning: and when the day began to spring, they let her go. Then came the woman in the dawning of the day, and fell down at the door of the man's house where her lord was, till it was light.
>
> —JUDGES 19:22, 25-26, KJV

The sons of Belial literally raped the concubine of the Levite to death. Rape is an evil that humiliates its victim, causing them to become defamed. Belial operates by depleting every single ounce of value and worth one has. In biblical times, when a woman was raped she could no longer marry. Considered a marked woman, her name was scarred. Her life became worthless because during those times women centered their lives on getting married and producing male sons. Second Samuel 13:11–13 gives an example of this. Tamar was raped by her brother Amnon and after being violated, became a recluse living in Absalom's home, a desolate woman. Desolate is defined as "barren, empty, and unfruitful."

While physical rape is a great evil taking place within the world today, spiritual rape is increasing immensely within the church. It is manifesting in barren bellies and lives that exhibit no fruit. Micah 2:8 says:

> Even of late my people is risen up as an enemy: ye pull off the robe with the garment from them that pass by securely as men averse from war.

—KJV

The definition of *rape* is "to destroy and strip of its possession." Those influenced by the spirit of Belial specializes in stripping the robes from the backs of God's people causing them to be exposed and ashamed. People within the kingdom of God are not walking worthy or stepping into God-given mantles because their wombs are being raped to death by ravenous wolves. They are being stripped of purpose and destiny because a spirit of death has been attached to them.

Furthermore, the body is being raped of the truth because truth is being stripped from the pulpit, from national platforms—this leads to bareness and barrenness. Barren wombs and empty cribs are not God's portion for us as His children. We are to be fruitful and we are to multiply in every aspect of our lives. Amos 3:7 says:

> Surely the Sovereign LORD does nothing without revealing his plan to his servants the prophets.

The Hebrew word for reveal is *galah* which means "to uncover, lay bare, denude, expose, or to strip." While the enemy uses false prophets to strip away the truth, the Lord uncovers His plans to the true prophets. He strips away the veils from their understanding so that they may know and discern the next move of God. God is always ahead of the Enemy and the spiritual rapists of this age will be exposed.

I dreamed of a woman who was preparing for a trip. While on the road headed to her destination, she remembered that she'd left something of importance behind. Upon returning home, she found an unknown male standing at her front door. The woman proceeded to use her house key to unlock the door, but the stranger insisted that she used his key instead. Looking down at his key, she saw that his was much bigger and shinier than hers. Because his key was more appealing, she allowed him to open the door using his. As they entered her home, the man followed her into the bedroom and raped her. After the incident, the young woman realized that her parents were in the room the whole time and did nothing to stop the attack. In fact, they were speaking kind words amongst each other as though nothing ever happened.

There are false spiritual parents and leaders among us who use their authority to intimidate others into believing that they are superior in knowledge, wisdom, and stature. Because of their position, they assume that they are better than everyone else and use their power to abuse individuals as they see fit. In this season, we must be careful about who we are letting into our house and whose house we are entering.

7. Intimidates the Young in God

And there are gathered unto him vain men, the children of Belial, and have strengthened themselves against Rehoboam the son of

Solomon, when Rehoboam was young and tenderhearted, and could not withstand them.

—2 CHRONICLES 13:7, KJV

The NIV version says that the sons of Belial struck "when Rehoboam was indecisive and not strong enough to resist them." The spirit of Belial attempts to intimidate the young in the Lord. They lure the indecisive and the weak in God into the arms of deception. The young are unable to break the influence of the leaders influenced by Belial because they are not yet strong in the Lord.

8. OPPOSES LEADERSHIP

But the children of Belial said, how shall this man save us? And they despised him, and brought no presents. But he held his peace

—1 SAMUEL 10:27, KJV

God positioned Saul as king after Israel rejected Him as their King and Groom. While Saul would eventually be rejected by God due to disobedience, he was still God's chosen at the time. Yet certain "children of Belial" chose to rise up against what God had ordained for that moment. Belial manifests by causing men to rise and rebel against authority, which is another attempt to destroy God's leadership.

The sons of Belial despised Saul. The Hebrew word for *despise* is *bazah*, meaning "to disesteem, disdain, to scorn." A scornful person is one who looks down on another in their lowly state. Thus, the spirit of Belial manifests itself by showing contempt toward leadership. Those influenced feel as though they "know better" or "have a better way." They believe their leaders are incapable of leading. This is a person with whom no one can reason; they become unapproachable and belligerent when corrected by leadership. They are foolish. First Samuel 25:3–6, 10 KJV, says:

> Now the name of the man was Nabal; and the name of his wife Abigail: and she was a woman of good understanding, and of a beautiful countenance: but the man was churlish and evil in his doings; and he was of the house of Caleb. And David heard in the wilderness that Nabal did shear his sheep. And David sent out ten young men, and David said unto the young men, Get you up to Carmel, and go to Nabal, and greet him in my name: And thus shall ye say to him that liveth in prosperity, Peace be both to thee, and peace be to thine house, and peace be unto all that thou hast.... And Nabal answered David's servants, and said, Who is David? And who is the son of Jesse? There be many servants now a days that break away every man from his master.

Nabal means "fool or senseless." Likewise, many have become fools, thinking that they can usurp authority without judgment. Influenced by the spirit of Belial blatantly they disrespect leadership. They are senseless and have allowed pride to cause them to err. Operating in sheer rebellion, they exclaim, "Who are you to tell me what to do?" Belial's vendetta is to bring down God's anointed by any means necessary; they scandalize, challenge, and even rebuke those in authority. The person influenced by this spirit is a gossiper and a slanderer among members causing division within the church. Some have even as gone as far as uprooting members from their place of worship when they decide to leave. They wield their tongues against the chosen of God which is no small thing because "Death and life are in the power of the tongue" (Prov. 18:21). When one speaks against the man or woman of God, seeds of death are planted that attempt to murder His ministry. But what God has ordained will stand despite onslaught from Satan.

Second Samuel 22:5–7 says:

> When the waves of death compassed me, the floods of ungodly men made me afraid; the sorrows of hell compassed me about; the snares of death prevented me; in my distress I called upon the LORD, and cried to my God: and he did hear my voice out of his temple, and my cry did enter into his ears.

—KJV

The literal translation for "when the waves of death compassed me," is "when the floods of Belial encompassed me." As the flood of Belial encompassed God's servant David, so has the flood of Belial been released upon the church, the body, and the nation as a whole. But "when the enemy comes in like a flood, God will raise a standard against him." (See Isaiah 59:19.)

A young man at the church I attend submitted a dream to me for interpretation. Inside of a sanctuary were people holding microphones and speaking all manner of evil things. A woman named Helen pointed and said, "Don't you see all the evil taking place here? Can't you hear what they are saying?" All of a sudden the earth split beneath them from the pulpit where they stood, to the lobby, and then outside of the front door. After hearing this dream

127

my mind immediately fell upon Numbers 16:1–3, 32-
33:

> Now Korah son of Izhar, the son of Kohath,
> the son of Levi, with Dathan and Abiram
> sons of Eliab, and On son of Peleth, sons of
> Reuben, took men, And they rose up before
> Moses, with certain of the Israelites, 250
> princes or leaders of the congregation called
> to the assembly, men well known and of
> distinction. And they gathered together
> against Moses and Aaron, and said to them,
> [Enough of you!] You take too much upon
> yourselves, seeing that all the congregation is
> holy, every one of them, and the Lord is
> among them. Why then do you lift yourselves
> up above the assembly of the Lord?....And the
> earth opened its mouth and swallowed them
> and their households and [Korah and] all [his]
> men and all their possessions. They and all
> that belonged to them went down alive into
> Sheol (the place of the dead); and the earth
> closed upon them, and they perished from
> among the assembly.

Korah influenced by the spirit of Belial,
convinced the congregation to stand against the
servant of God out of rebellion. I was also led to
Psalm 74:4–8, which says:

> In the midst of Your Holy Place Your
> enemies have roared [with their battle cry];
> they set up their own [idol] emblems for signs
> [of victory]. They seemed like men who lifted
> up axes upon a thicket of trees to make
> themselves a record. And then all the carved
> wood of the Holy Place they broke down with
> hatchets and hammers. They have set Your
> sanctuary on fire; they have profaned the
> dwelling place of Your Name by casting it to

the ground. They said in their hearts, Let us make havoc [of such places] altogether. They have burned up all God's meetinghouses in the land.

The interpretation of the dream is clear. There are people of influence (microphones) in the body of Christ who have begun to carry out and perform lewd acts right in the midst of God's house. As sons of Belial, they act contemptuously in outright rebellion. God, however, is about to shed light (meaning of the name Helen) upon the acts of harlotry within His church. He will remove blasphemers from the pulpit and place them outside of the exit door. He will clear national platforms of "sons of Belial." He is going to separate the right from the wrong, the true from the false, and the sons of God from the sons of Belial.

129

6

THE SPIRIT *of* LUST

> For all that is in the world--the lust of the
> flesh [craving for sensual gratification] and the
> lust of the eyes [greedy longings of the mind]
> and the pride of life [assurance in one's own
> resources or in the stability of earthly things]--
> these do not come from the Father but are
> from the world [itself].
>
> —1 JOHN 2:16

L UST IS TYPICALLY a word used to describe
unfeigned sexual attraction toward a person
who is off-limits. It is "an overwhelming desire
or craving, an intense or obsessive desire, especially
one that is sexual." While accurate descriptions, those
definitions barely scrape the surface, because sexual
gratification is only one of the many manifestations of
the spirit of lust. Lust is much deeper than sex.

The Greek word for *lust* used in the New
Testament is *epithymeo*, which means "to set the heart
upon and to long for (rightfully or otherwise)." Lust
can either be good or bad. In fact, *lust*, *covet*, and *desire*
are synonymous in the Greek and the Hebrew.

We are instructed in the Word of God to *covet* the best gifts. (See 1 Corinthians 12:31.) We are also told that God will give us the *desires* (lusts) of our hearts. (See Psalm 37:4.) Many misconstrue this verse to mean that God will give us the desires of our wicked hearts; this could not be further from the truth. God gives us the lusts of our hearts once His desire becomes our desire.

If the object of desire is God, then the heart is set upon and eagerly yearns after Him, but when the heart lusts after ungodly things, an idol is erected inside the heart. Thus, lust snares the heart long before it snares the flesh and is the manifestation of what is already happening inside the heart of the offender. "Whosoever looketh on a woman to lust after her hath committed adultery with her already in his heart" (Matt. 5:28, KJV). The Book of Genesis depicts the first account of heart disease.

> But the serpent said to the woman, you shall not surely die, For God knows that in the day you eat of it your eyes will be opened, and you will be like God, knowing the difference between good and evil and blessing and calamity. And when the woman saw that the tree was good (suitable, pleasant) for food and that it was delightful to look at, and a tree to be desired in order to make one wise, she took of its fruit and ate.

—GENESIS 3:4–6

While it is true that Satan is a master of trickery, Eve allowed him to appeal to the lust of her flesh— "the woman saw that the tree was good (suitable, pleasant) for food," the lust of her eyes—"it was delightful to look at," and the pride of life—"it was a tree to be desired in order to make one wise." There was something inside of the hearts of Eve and Adam that matched the evil Satan presented in the Garden. Lust was merely a symptom of their heart disease. That day, Adam and Eve introduced the knowledge of good and evil to the world and hearts have been turning ever since.

AHOLAH AND AHOLIBAH

And the names of them were Aholah the elder and Aholibah her sister, and they became Mine and they bore sons and daughters. As for the identity of their names, Aholah is Samaria and Aholibah is Jerusalem. And Aholah played the harlot when she was Mine, and she was foolishly fond of her lovers and doted on the Assyrians her neighbors, Who were clothed with blue, governors and deputies, all of them attractive young men, horsemen riding upon horses. And she bestowed her harlotries upon them, the choicest men of Assyria all of them; and on whomever she doted, with all their idols she defiled herself....These uncovered her nakedness and shame; they took her sons and her daughters and they slew her with the sword, and her name became notorious and a byword among women when judgments were executed upon her.

—EZEKIEL 23:4–7, 10

Above is a parable of Samaria and Jerusalem who were guilty of playing the harlot against God with Egypt, Assyria, and Babylonia. Samaria was given the name Aholah, which means "her own tabernacle." This suggests that Samaria was guilty of creating her own religion because God was not in the establishment of their religious organization. It was of their own will. Even though they belonged to God, they created Assyrian gods to rival Him. She "doted" on her lovers based upon their physical attractiveness; they were young and handsome. Clothed in blue, they had the appearance of wealth and prosperity. Impressed by positions and titles (governors, deputies, and officers), she deemed them more sufficient to provide for and protect her than God. Harlotry was at the core of the people of Samaria, and like Eve and Gomer, all it took was opportunity to reveal the lust of their hearts.

> And her sister Aholibah saw this; yet she was more corrupt in her foolish fondness than she, and in her harlotries she was more wanton than her sister in her harlotries. She doted upon the Assyrians--governors and deputies, her neighbors, clothed most gorgeously, horsemen riding upon horses, all of them desirable young men. And I saw that she was defiled, that both [of the sisters] took one way. But [Aholibah] carried her harlotries further, for she saw men pictured upon the wall, the pictures of the Chaldeans sketched in bright red pigment, Girded with girdles on their loins, with flowing turbans on their heads, all of them looking like officers, a picture of Babylonian men whose native land was Chaldea, Then as soon as she saw [the sketches of] them, she doted on them and sent messengers to them in Chaldea.

> —EZEKIEL 23:11–16

Jerusalem was referred to as Aholibah, which means "my tabernacle is in her." God's temple was in Jerusalem and as a groom gives his bride his last name, so did God acknowledge Jerusalem by putting

His name on them. Yet, they were considered more corrupt than Samaria. They should have learned from the mistakes of Samaria, but instead became infatuated with the Egyptians and the Babylonians. Jerusalem even went as far as to lust after images and paintings portrayed on the walls. Like Samaria, the Egyptians grabbed her heart because they had the image of wealth, prosperity, and strength. She lusted for them because in her eyes, they were men of great importance and protection. Hence, she formed an alliance with them, when it was God who truly loved her.

> And the Babylonians came to her into the bed of love, and they defiled her with their evil desire; and when she was polluted by them, she [Jerusalem] broke the relationship and pushed them away from her in disgust. So she flaunted her harlotries and exposed her nakedness, and I was disgusted and turned from her, as I had turned in disgust from her sister.
>
> —Ezekiel 23:17-18

Pollution is defined as "being contaminated with harmful substances as a consequence of human activities, the condition of being impure, defilement, and adulteration." Jerusalem had become defiled by her indiscretions. The Egyptians and Babylonians had adulterated the people of God and as a result, they became impure.

> The word of the Lord came again to me, saying, Son of man, there were two women, the daughters of one mother; And they played the harlot in Egypt. There they played the harlot in their youth; there their bosoms were

135

pressed and there their virgin breasts were
handled.

—EZEKIEL 23:1–3

In a dream, I watched young women who stood
behind a wall in a field with their breasts exposed.
Their sole purpose was to entice the young men who
stood nearby. The men weren't innocent by any
means, because when they saw the women, they ran
to peek over the wall to watch them in their
nakedness. Continuing to act shamelessly, the young
women did nothing to cover up.

The Hebrew word for "breast" is *shad*. Breasts are
symbolic of nourishment and provision. God is El
Shaddai, which is translated the "Many Breasted
One." He is El Shaddai because He is sufficient in
supplying the needs of His people. He alone is the all-
sufficient One; He is God Almighty. However, many
within the body of Christ have begun to run and peek
over the walls, lusting after falsity that appeases them
at the peak of their sinful desire.

Just as Jerusalem lusted after paintings on walls,
we have become master painters and are guilty of
lusting after images. In ancient times, paint was what
we refer to today as make-up or cosmetics. Cosmetics
are applied to the face in order to improve or alter the
appearance. Imperfections are covered up in order to
be appealing and pleasing to the eyes of the
beholders.

A beautiful "made-up" lie has also been set before
the multitudes, one that is based upon individualistic
desires; one that chooses which parts of the gospel
that is appealing and covers up that which is
considered undesirable. Satan has infiltrated minds all

across the globe with false doctrine, making it pleasing to the flesh according to the world's standards. It's an easy gospel, one full of lies but one that's lusted after because it promises wealth in the midst of sin, it cries out peace when there is no peace, and prophesies rain while in the midst of a God-ordained drought. Like Jezebel's, we paint our own eyes so that we may hide from the truth. (See 2 Kings 9:30 and Ezekiel 23:40).

Professing Christian leaders take the meat of the Word of God and prepare it vegan for the vegetarians, fruit for clean eaters and cake for those with a sweet tooth. We as the body of Christ have been guilty of creating false gods of our own imagination. We paint God into a false image that satisfies our sinful lust and cravings. When we preach a false gospel, one that takes away from who God truly is, we are guilty of idolatry because any god preached outside of the inerrant Word of God is a graven image. False prophets of the world are masters of deception. They are whitewashed (painted over) as described in Matthew 23:23–28:

> Woe to you, scribes and Pharisees, pretenders (hypocrites)! For you clean the outside of the cup and of the plate, but within they are full of extortion (prey, spoil, plunder) and grasping self-indulgence. You blind Pharisee! First clean the inside of the cup and of the plate, so that the outside may be clean also. Woe to you, scribes and Pharisees, pretenders (hypocrites)! For you are like tombs that have been whitewashed, which look beautiful on the outside but inside are full of dead men's bones and everything impure. Just so, you also outwardly seem to people to be just and

upright but inside you are full of pretense and
lawlessness and iniquity.

In a dream, I watched a baby as he sat in a high
chair with a plate of food before him. Ironically,
instead of placing the food into his mouth, he placed
spoonfuls of food into his eyes.

There are many spiritual babies within the body of
Christ who are constantly trying to feed the lust of
their eyes. First Corinthians 3:1–3 says:

> However, brethren, I could not talk to you as
> to spiritual [men], but as to nonspiritual [men
> of the flesh, in whom the carnal nature
> predominates], as to mere infants [in the new
> life] in Christ [unable to talk yet!] I fed you
> with milk, not solid food, for you were not yet
> strong enough [to be ready for it]; but even
> yet you are not strong enough [to be ready for
> it], For you are still [unspiritual, having the
> nature] of the flesh [under the control of
> ordinary impulses]. For as long as [there are]
> envying and jealousy and wrangling and
> factions among you, are you not unspiritual
> and of the flesh, behaving yourselves after a
> human standard and like mere (unchanged)
> men?

Spiritual infants have no desire to be fed the truth
and as a result, have no desire to grow. Lusting after
false prophets who speak from their own hearts,
causes a growth stunt. Many have become more
preoccupied with positions, titles, prosperity, and
wealth than they have with spiritual maturity. The
body cannot be nourished upon anything outside of
the truth, which is the unadulterated Word of God.
Anything else results in a body that is starving to
death.

We must not believe the lie of the Enemy which says there is sufficiency outside of God. We must not dethrone God and replace Him with our own works. We must not flaunt our breasts (self-sufficiency), in the face of an Almighty God. "Thus says the Lord cursed [with great evil] is the strong man who trusts in and relies on frail man, making weak [human] flesh his arm, and whose mind and heart turn aside from the Lord" (Jer. 17:5).

JUDGMENT

> Therefore, O Aholibah, thus says the Lord God: Behold, I will rouse up your lovers against you, from whom you turned in disgust, and I will bring them against you on every side: The Babylonians and all the Chaldeans, Pekod and Shoa and Koa, and all the Assyrians with them, desirable young men, governors and officers all of them, princes, men of renown and counselors, all of them riding on horses. And they shall come against you with weapons, chariots, wagons and wheels, and with a host of infantry which shall array themselves against you with buckler and shield and helmet round about; and I will commit the judgment and punishment to them, and they shall judge and punish you according to their [heathen] customs in such matters. And I will set My jealous indignation against you, and they shall deal with you in fury; they shall take away your nose and your ears, and those who are left of you shall fall by the sword; they shall take your sons and your daughters, and the remainder shall be devoured by the fire.

—EZEKIEL 23:22–25

During biblical times, it was customary for those who were caught in adultery to have their noses and ears removed to their jealous husbands. Marked by this disfigurement, they were known to others not as who they were, but by what they did. Why the nose and the ears? Genesis 2:7 says:

> Then the Lord God formed man from the dust of the ground and breathed into his nostrils the breath or spirit of life, and man became a living being.

The nose is where God breathed life into every living human being. Without the breath that God gives, there is only death. As read earlier, Samaria and Jerusalem "doted" after the idolatrous nations. *Doted* in the Hebrew is "agab" which is translated "to breathe after." The nose is also mentioned in Ezekiel 8:17, which says:

> Then [the Spirit] said to me, Have you seen this, O son of man? Is it too slight a thing to the house of Judah to commit the abominations which they commit here, that they must fill the land with violence and turn back afresh to provoke Me to anger? And behold, they put the branch to their nose [actually, before their mouths, in superstitious worship]!

The *Bible Encyclopedia* states that the phrase "branch to the nose" alludes to a rite connected with the worship of Baal (the sun). In similar Persian sun worship, a bunch of dates, pomegranates, or tamarisks were held to the nose by the worshipper, probably as an attempt to keep the holy one (sun) from being contaminated by sinful breath. The nose was used as a means to pledge allegiance to the false god Baal.[14]

The people of God were guilty of breathing after the things of the world. The very breath that God gave to them, they used to breathe life into falsehood. Thus, cutting off the nose was symbolic of cutting off life. For us, it represents a spiritual death.

> But they would not listen to and obey Me or bend their ear [to Me], but followed the counsels and the stubborn promptings of their own evil hearts and minds, and they turned their backs and went in reverse instead of forward.
>
> —JEREMIAH 7:24

The judgment of the cutting off of the ears is simple. Because they refused to hear the Word of the Lord, He removed the tools used to pledge allegiance to their worthless trinkets of metal and iron.

We too are approaching a season when God is about to cut the spiritually dead off the body because "the wages of sin is death."(See Romans 6:23.) Those who God will use in this season will be marked by His anointing, but those lusting after the world will be marked by the disfigurement of their transgressions. All will discern that the power of God is no longer flowing through their lives because they have "set their nose to the branch." Stripped bare from all they lusted after, they will be brought low leaving them in a posture of prayer for repentance and growth.

Hebrews 5:12–14 says:

> For even though by this time you ought to be teaching others, you actually need someone to teach you over again the very first principles of God's Word. You have come to need milk, not solid food. For everyone who continues to feed on milk is obviously inexperienced

> and unskilled in the doctrine of righteousness (of conformity to the divine will in purpose, thought, and action), for he is a mere infant [not able to talk yet]! But solid food is for full-grown men, for those whose senses and mental faculties are trained by practice to discriminate and distinguish between what is morally good and noble and what is evil and contrary either to divine or human law.

It is time for the body of Christ to grow up and to mature. We must leave behind the lust of the flesh, of the eyes and the pride of life, which leads to death. We must turn our desires toward God and begin to seek hard after Him again. Jesus came so that we would have life more abundantly, but according to His desires and His will, not our lust. (See John 10:10.)

> For the desires of the flesh are opposed to the [Holy] Spirit, and the [desires of the] Spirit are opposed to the flesh (godless human nature); for these are antagonistic to each other [continually withstanding and in conflict with each other], so that you are not free but are prevented from doing what you desire to do.

—GALATIANS 5:17

142

7

THE SPIRIT *of* PRIDE

I know Ephraim, and Israel is not hid from
Me; for now, O Ephraim, you have played the
harlot and have worshiped idols; Israel is
defiled. Their doings will not permit them to
return to their God, for the spirit of harlotry
is within them and they know not the Lord
[they do not recognize, appreciate, give heed
to, or cherish the Lord]. But the pride and
self-reliance of Israel testifies before his [own]
face. Therefore shall [all] Israel, and
[especially] Ephraim [the northern ten tribes],
totter and fall in their iniquity and guilt, and
Judah shall stumble and fall with them.

—HOSEA 5:3–5

ONE NIGHT I dreamed of acrobats gracefully
performing and cascading from the roof of a
large circus tent. High and lifted up, at the
peak of excellence, they swung from side to side,
accomplishing amazing feats in strides of elegance. I
recall how effortless it appeared, though I was certain
that their flawless execution was evidence of
countless hours spent in training and cultivating the
gift. However, in the midst their performance, the

acrobats fell suddenly from the sky at rapid speed; and worse, I saw that there was no safety net below to catch them. Although I didn't witness the acrobats plummet to the ground, I was awakened from the dream by the sound of a loud crash, like fireworks exploding on the Fourth of July.

An acrobat in defined in two ways: first as "an entertainer who performs acts that require skill, agility, and coordination, such as tumbling, swinging from a trapeze, or walking a tightrope" and also as "a person noted for frequent and rapid changes of position or allegiances." An acrobat is one with the ability to contort the body and perform a series of tricks in front of an audience. They are said to "walk on the extremity." In other words, they have learned to walk in unnatural and inherently unbalanced manners for the sake of pleasing an audience. An acrobat would generally have to be extremely strong, flexible, and highly creative in order to develop new movements that are enjoyable to their audience. Their ability to perform lies in their strength; their ability to balance lies in their legs. For their own safety, they are warned not to look down, but to continuously look ahead.

What does this dream have to do with pride? Much like the acrobats in the dream, there are many spiritual acrobats who are lifted high above audiences in noticeably visible positions. Many eyes are upon them as they sit upon highly recognized platforms. They command the attention of a crowd with sideshow tricks. They have mastered the art of performing, contorting the body as they swing from one extreme to the next. These new movements that are arising did not originate with God. The spiritual acrobat's methods are unnatural; they have an imbalanced perception and declaration of the Word of God. They have begun to transform the house of God into a three-ring circus.

The word *contort* means "to bend severely out of shape, to deform, distort, to morph, or to warp." The imbalanced and unnatural way that the Word of God is handled in this hour is responsible for distorting the truth and thereby deforming the body. Ephesians 4:12–13 says:

> His intention was the perfecting and the full equipping of the saints (His consecrated people), [that they should do] the work of ministering toward building up Christ's body (the church), [That it might develop] until we all attain oneness in the faith and in the comprehension of the [full and accurate] knowledge of the Son of God, that [we might arrive] at really mature manhood (the completeness of personality which is nothing less than the standard height of Christ's own perfection), the measure of the stature of the fullness of the Christ and the completeness found in Him.

The creation of "new movements" in an effort to entertain and please audiences has become more important than growth. While God's intention for preaching the Word is for perfecting the saints, many have begun to perfect their performances instead. The people of God have become captivated by the next new movement, the next new prophetic word of prosperity, the next new conference, and the next "new fire." Attention is being lifted away from God and placed upon side shows. The church is guilty of falling in love with beautifully, well orchestrated performances. Second Timothy 4:3–4 says:

> For the time is coming when [people] will not tolerate (endure) sound and wholesome instruction, but, having ears itching [for something pleasing and gratifying], they will gather to themselves one teacher after another to a considerable number, chosen to satisfy their own liking and to foster the errors they hold, And will turn aside from hearing the truth and wander off into myths and man-made fictions.

Pride is the most frequently used tool of Satan and is defined as "an excessively high opinion of oneself." However, pride it is much deeper than mere arrogance. Pride is when one substitutes their own authority, strength, will, plan, purpose, desires, or human goodness in the place of God's. In essence, pride boasts, "I am as wise as God." Pride tells the Creator what to do with His creation; it began and ends with Satan. Ezekiel 28:11–13 reads:

> Moreover, the word of the Lord came to me, saying, Son of man, take up a lamentation over the king of Tyre and say to him, thus says the Lord God: You are the full measure and pattern of exactness [giving the finishing touch to all that constitutes completeness], full of wisdom and perfect in beauty._You were in Eden, the garden of God; every precious stone was your covering, the carnelian, topaz, jasper, chrysolite, beryl, onyx, sapphire, carbuncle, and emerald; and your settings and your sockets *and* engravings were wrought in gold. On the day that you were created they were prepared.

Satan was the most beautiful of all God's creation. He was the "sum," meaning he was given the complete measure of beauty. He was covered in every beautiful precious stone to be imagined. Satan was given the very best by the Lord but became utterly deceived into thinking he could take God's place. This is exactly how pride seeks to destroy us as the children of God. God blesses with gifts, talents, and abilities and then the Enemy sneaks in with pride to pervert the very blessings God has given.

Many have become obsessed with the "great name" they've made for themselves. Focus is placed upon building ministries versus building the church. They have taken the very wisdom of God and counted it as foolishness. Religious church programs full of tradition, exegesis, and theatrics have replaced the presence of God. Room is not allowed for the move of the Spirit, and the flow of God has been quenched and trumped by prolonged, eloquent messages that sound good but have no demonstration of power. Church services have become meaningless, fruitless, and man-centered. Sadly, worship services are now considered as just another "event" or a place to view live entertainment. Ezekiel 28:14 continues:

> You were the anointed cherub that covers with overshadowing [wings], and I set you so. You were upon the holy mountain of God; you walked up and down in the midst of the stones of fire [like the paved work of gleaming sapphire stone upon which the God of Israel walked on Mount Sinai].

Satan was anointed and ordained as one who "covered." Given a lofty position, he had unlimited access to the presence of God. Likewise, leaders today

147

have been given, by the authority of God, the charge of covering and protecting His people. The responsibility of the shepherd is to gather and feed the flock of God. However, the children of God are not being fed, but led astray by empty, vain messages inflated with pride and egotism. Still these leaders use their position and authority in God to further manipulate and deceive people into treating them like gods. The image of man has become enshrined in the hearts of the multitudes where only God belongs. This is a form of idolatry and is highly dangerous. The worship of man is nothing new; it is an age-old sin that continues to thrive today. The apostle Paul speaks of the worship of images in Romans 1:21–23, which says:

> Because when they knew and recognized Him as God, they did not honor and glorify Him as God or give Him thanks. But instead they became futile and godless in their thinking [with vain imaginings, foolish reasoning, and stupid speculations] and their senseless minds were darkened. Claiming to be wise, they became fools [professing to be smart, they made simpletons of themselves]. And by them the glory and majesty and excellence of the immortal God were exchanged for and represented by images, resembling mortal man and birds and beasts and reptiles.

Satan uses pride to strip the call of God from the lives of His people. This is evident in the life of Sampson, who had a sweet tooth for harlots. Sampson continuously fell victim to the seductive schemes of Delilah until the day he awoke, shook himself, and realized that the power of God had lifted from his life. Prior to this, when asked where his

The Spirit of Pride

strength lied, he said that it was in his hair. He had forgotten that his power was from God and his strength was in God. Thus when his hair was cut off, so was his power.

Many leaders, like the acrobats discussed earlier, have accredited their strength and anointing to their own legs. They have become possessive laying claim to the anointing of God making statements such as "my call" or "my anointing." But if their anointing originated with Jesus, it belongs to Him alone. In these final days, many will awake and shake themselves, sadly realizing that their heads are bald because the anointing of God no longer flows in their lives.

Proverbs 16:18 says, "Pride goes before destruction and a haughty spirit before a fall." In the dream, the acrobats in all of their beauty and grace, agility, and strength, fell to the ground where there was no net, much like the fall of Satan when God cast him to the ground from heaven. The higher one is lifted in pride, the lower he shall go and the greater the shame. King Nebuchadnezzar is a prime example of how pride eventually brings those in even the highest of positions back down to earth.

Daniel 4:24–26 gives the interpretation of a dream that King Nebuchadnezzar had about himself:

> This is the interpretation, O king: It is the decree of the Most High [God] which has come upon my lord the king .You shall be driven from among men and your dwelling shall be with the beasts of the field; you shall be made to eat grass as do the oxen and you shall be wet with the dew of the heavens; and seven times [or years] shall pass over you until you learn and know and recognize that the

149

> Most High [God] rules the kingdom of mankind and gives it to whomever He will. And in that it was commanded to leave the stump of the roots of the tree, your kingdom shall be sure to you after you have learned and know that [the God of] heaven rules.

Nebuchadnezzar was famous and self-sufficient, or so he thought. Everything he thought he needed, he already had and could reproduce if need be. He foolishly assumed his earthly, humanistic wisdom to be comparable to, or greater than God's. Daniel 4: 27-28 says:

> Therefore, O king, let my counsel be acceptable to you; break off your sins and show the reality of your repentance by righteousness (right standing with God and moral and spiritual rectitude and rightness in every area and relation) and liberate yourself from your iniquities by showing mercy and loving-kindness to the poor and oppressed, that [if the king will repent] there may possibly be a continuance and lengthening of your peace and tranquility and a healing of your error. All this was fulfilled and came upon King Nebuchadnezzar.

Even after the interpretation of the dream was given by Daniel, Nebuchadnezzar refused to repent. Instead, the spirit of pride stood up in him and replied, "Is not this the great Babylon that I have built as the royal residence and seat of government by the might of my power and for the honor and glory of my majesty?" As a result of Nebuchadnezzar's blasphemy, God spoke from heaven, declaring that the kingdom had departed from him. At the very moment the word was spoken, Nebuchadnezzar was driven away. He totally lost his mind, the very thing he treasured and put his strength in. For seven years he grazed around as an animal in the fields. He wouldn't fall to his knees in repentance, so God brought him to his knees by ways of trial and difficulty. It was upon his knees that he discovered that God was God. Look at what Daniel 4:34, 37 says:

> And at the end of the days [seven years], I, Nebuchadnezzar, lifted up my eyes to heaven, and my understanding and the right use of my mind returned to me; and I blessed the Most High [God] and I praised and honored and glorified Him Who lives forever, Whose dominion is an everlasting dominion; and His kingdom endures from generation to generation…. Now I, Nebuchadnezzar, praise and extol and honor the King of heaven, whose works are all faithful and right and Whose ways are just. And those who walk in pride He is able to abase and humble.

Sadly, it is true that many would never look up unless they were cast down. Humility is much needed in this hour because "If anyone desires to be first, he must be last of all, and servant of all" (Mark 9:35). Ezekiel 28:17–18 continues:

> Your heart was proud and lifted up because of your beauty; you corrupted your wisdom for the sake of your splendor. I cast you to the ground; I lay you before kings that they might gaze at you. You have profaned your sanctuaries by the multitude of your iniquities and the enormity of your guilt, by the unrighteousness of your trade. Therefore I have brought forth a fire from your midst; it has consumed you, and I have reduced you to ashes upon the earth in the sight of all who looked at you.

God is reminding us today that there is no higher place than at His feet. In an effort to save those who have fallen in pride, He is going to remove them from their high places. In order to humble them and to bring forth repentance, He will bring them low. Satan's ultimate goal is to cause a great fall of the leaders and members in the body of Christ, because his fall is inevitable. While there is no safety net for him, we as the children of God have the chance to repent and turn our hearts back to Him.

> But He gives us more and more grace (power of the Holy Spirit, to meet this evil tendency and all others fully). That is why He says, God sets Himself against the proud and haughty, but gives grace [continually] to the lowly (those who are humble enough to receive it)….[As you draw near to God] be deeply penitent and grieve, even weep [over your disloyalty]. Let your laughter be turned to grief and your mirth to dejection and heartfelt shame [for your sins]. Humble yourselves [feeling very insignificant] in the presence of the Lord, and He will exalt you [He will lift you up and make your lives significant].
>
> —JAMES 4:6, 9–10

8

THE SPIRIT *of* MAMMON

Riches and honor are with me, enduring
wealth and righteousness (uprightness in every
area and relation, and right standing with
God). My fruit is better than gold, yes, than
refined gold, and my increase than choice
silver. I [Wisdom] walk in the way of
righteousness (moral and spiritual rectitude in
every area and relation), in the midst of the
paths of justice, that I may cause those who
love me to inherit [true] riches and that I may
fill their treasuries.

—PROVERBS 8:18–21

MANY RAISE EYEBROWS or suspicions when
they feel as though Christians live lifestyles
that are considered extravagant. Religion
has many believing that wealth is ungodly and
unbiblical. While I do feel as though some become
frivolous and careless, using riches wickedly, I am also
very much aware that we cannot serve Jehovah Jireh
without being provided for. Contrary to popular
belief, God does not wish for His children to be
impoverished in any area of our lives. If we are the

seed of Abraham, and children of the King of Kings, then there is no reason for us to believe that we are called to be poor. In fact, He blesses us so that we can give extravagantly to those in need. First Timothy 6:17-19 says:

> As for the rich in this world, charge them not to be proud *and* arrogant *and* contemptuous of others, nor to set their hopes on uncertain riches, but on God, Who richly *and* ceaselessly provides us with everything for [our] enjoyment. [Charge them] to do good, to be rich in good works, to be liberal *and* generous of heart, ready to share [with others],In this way laying up for themselves [the riches that endure forever as] a good foundation for the future, so that they may grasp that which is life indeed.

God has nothing against true wealth. In fact, as Christians, He has given to us the power to obtain it. (See Deuteronomy 8:18.) We have a treasure inside of our earthen vessels, which means the almighty God lives on the inside of us and with Him comes purpose, blessings, and wealth. (See 2 Corinthians 4:7.)

However, many have misconstrued what constitutes true wealth; this does not exclude the body of Christ. It is evident that we are living in the perilous times that have been spoken of, because truly men have become lovers of money and will do any and everything in order to obtain it. (See 2 Timothy 3.) Greed is one of the many characteristics of the spirit of harlotry because, as we know, a harlot does debase things in order to gain financial security. Spiritual harlots are no different in that they sink to new lows in an effort to reach what they deem as new heights of "success." The mind-set of the people of God has become warped by false messages that promote prosperity without righteousness. Matthew 6:24 says:

> No one can serve two masters; for either he will hate the one and love the other, or he will stand by and be devoted to the one and despise and be against the other. You cannot serve God and mammon (deceitful riches, money, possessions, or whatever is trusted in).

Money has the potential to be worshiped; therefore, it also has the potential to become an idol inside of the heart. As previously discussed, the children of Israel were all too familiar with this. They were guilty of looking enviously at neighboring pagan countries, lusting after their wealth. In their minds idolatry reaped far greater benefits than waiting on God to supply their needs.

This sounds familiar in that many so called Christians have not learned anything from Israel's whoredom. Many regard the wealth of the world as greater than God's. We transform the Word of God into get-rich-quick schemes and then present them as the gospel. Micah 1:7 warns:

> And all her carved images shall be broken in pieces, and all her hires [all that man would gain from desertion of God] shall be burned with fire, and all her idols will be laid waste; for from the hire of [one] harlot she gathered them, and to the hire of [another] harlot they shall return.

All material possessions gained outside of the will of God leads to death. Our confidence should be placed in God and in Him alone. He is the Source, not our riches.

Mammon[15] is translated as, "confidence, wealth, personified, avarice (deified)." *Avarice* is defined as "reprehensible acquisitiveness, insatiable desire for wealth." Avarice is insatiable, meaning it's impossible to satisfy. So mammon is a spirit with the insatiable desire to always obtain more. It is often the driving force behind greed and lust. Mammon causes notable business associates and outstanding members of society to go to prison for embezzlement. It is the passion behind war, the instigator of divorce, and even murder. There is an insatiable desire to get more, and the end is destruction because when wealth is obtained and the quest is over, their reason for living is too. This is why many who are wealthy in material possessions still commit suicide; there was a void within them that could not be filled with material possessions. It could only be filled by God. Ezekiel 16:28–34 says:

> You played the harlot also with the Assyrians because you were unsatiable; yes, you played the harlot with them, and yet you were not satisfied. Moreover, you multiplied your harlotry with the land of trade, with Chaldea, and yet even with this you were not satisfied. How weak and spent with longing and lust is your heart and mind, says the Lord God, seeing you do all these things, the work of a bold, domineering harlot, In that you build your vaulted place (brothel) at the head of every street and make your high place at every crossing. But you were not like a harlot because you scorned pay. Rather, you were as an adulterous wife who receives strangers instead of her husband! Men give gifts to all harlots, but you give your gifts to all your lovers and hire them, bribing [the nations to

ally themselves with you], that they may come to you on every side for your harlotries (your idolatrous unfaithfulnesses to God). And you are different [the reverse] from other women in your harlotries, in that nobody follows you to lure you into harlotry and in that you give hire when no hire is given you; and so you are different.

In the text above, Israel is described as insatiable, yet they had become so corrupt that they no longer took material possessions from their neighboring countries. Instead, Israel gave them their possessions. They were influenced by immorality so much that they paid the neighboring countries to become their allies.

The insatiable desire for material wealth is a mere distraction from the greater underlying evil motivation of the spirit of mammon. Mammon is said to be the Syrian "god of riches" and originated from Babylon. Another word used to define mammon is *deified*, which means "to make a god of." The spirit of mammon along with pride is what influenced Nimrod to spearhead the construction of the Tower of Babel. Remember, Nimrod built the tower in order to become deified. The motivation behind constructing the tower was to ascend into a high place to replace God.

Babylon is the center of false doctrine and because mammon plays an integral part in its construction. This tells me that mammon causes a ravenous desire to obtain spiritual knowledge. In the natural realm, it appears to be a war after materialistic possessions, but in the realm of the spirit, there is a battle over spiritual wealth. "For we are not wrestling with flesh and blood [contending only with physical opponents], but against the despotisms, against the powers, against [the master spirits who are] the world rulers of this present darkness, against the spirit forces of wickedness in the heavenly (supernatural) sphere" (Ephesians 6:12).

Because Babylon constructed the false belief system, those used by the spirit of mammon can excel in what they consider "spiritual wealth" and lead the multitudes astray. Nimrod's tower was not built in order to obtain material wealth; on the contrary, it was built so that they could "make names for themselves." The spirit of mammon has many so far intertwined into the false Babylonian system of doctrine that they have lost their way. First Timothy 6:10 says:

> For the love of money is a root of all evils; it is through this craving that some have been led astray and have wandered from the faith and pierced themselves through with many acute [mental] pangs.

"Many have wandered away from the faith" is translated as "been seduced." Mammon comes to slip us away from the Bridegroom. Its ultimate goal is to turn hearts away from God. Luke 16:9, 13–15 says:

> And I tell you, make friends for yourselves by means of unrighteous mammon deceitful riches, money, possessions), so that when it fails, they [those you have favored] may receive and welcome you into the everlasting habitations (dwellings)....No servant is able to serve two masters; for either he will hate the one and love the other, or he will stand by and be devoted to the one and despise the other. You cannot serve God and mammon (riches, or anything in which you trust and on

which you rely). Now the Pharisees, who were covetous and lovers of money, heard all these things [taken together], and they began to sneer at and ridicule and scoff at Him. But He said to them, You are the ones who declare yourselves just and upright before men, but God knows your hearts. For what is exalted and highly thought of among men is detestable and abhorrent (an abomination) in the sight of God.

The Pharisees were hypocritical and vain. Heavily influenced by the spirit of mammon, they were guilty of tossing coins into the tray so that those nearby would hear it. They placed higher value on what man thought of them and less about what God already knew. Therefore, Scripture regards them as "covetous and lovers of money." Proverbs 13:11 says:

Wealth [not earned but] won in haste or unjustly or from the production of things for vain or detrimental use [such riches] will dwindle away, but he who gathers little by little will increase [his riches].

While the wealth of the world is temporal, there is a greater wealth that we as the people of God should seek after. We must not become so distracted by temporal pleasures that we forsake the eternal things, the spiritual wealth of God. The spirit of mammon has caused many to take on the mentality of Nimrod, which says "let us build so that we can have great names."

The spirit of mammon has caused the physical church to become idols in our hearts. The church has taken on this mentality in that we are preoccupied with building and beautifying our physical sanctuaries, while the world is decaying and dying. There are churches on nearly every street corner, yet an

overabundance of sickness, disease, and famine.
There are ministries on every block, yet people are
not being set free. Why? The Spirit of God has not
called them, the spirit of mammon has.   With
that said, many have no true revelation of what wealth
is. Wealth is defined as "the state of being rich and
affluent; having a plentiful supply of material goods
and money." However, the world's way of defining
wealth and God's way are two very different ideas.
Deuteronomy 8:18 reads:

> But you shall [earnestly] remember the Lord
> your God, for it is He Who gives you power
> to get wealth that He may establish His
> covenant which He swore to your fathers, as
> it is this day.

"Wealth" as it is used here is from the Hebrew
word *chayil*[16]. *Chayil* is mentioned over 200 times in
the Word of God and is interpreted as "strength,
might, efficiency, army, and force." Zechariah 4:6
says:

> So he answered and said to me "This *is* the
> word of the LORD to Zerubbabel 'Not by
> might nor by power, but by My Spirit, says the
> LORD of hosts.

The word *might* used above is also translated *chayil*.
It must be understood that wealth is not limited to
riches alone. We must also realize that we have no
power in ourselves to create true wealth or produce
anything worthwhile outside of the Spirit of God.
True wealth encompasses a multitude of blessings
from the Lord by the Lord. It includes strength, the
ability to withstand in times of trouble, the might and
the power to live right amid sheer chaos, efficiency in

all that we do, and the ability to be effective at whatever we put our hands to. True wealth from God is protected as an army protects its country, the enemy is not allowed to come into our camp and steal what God has given. True wealth is a force from God against the forces of evil. What God has blessed no man has the power to curse. (See Numbers 23:8.) Riches are not merely materialistic only. One can have great riches in the bank but be physically or spiritually ill and thus bankrupt. Wealth is not limited to cars, homes, jewelry, or cash.

In a vision, I watched the busy streets of a metropolitan area. People were preoccupied, looking down at their expensive watches, got into their new cars, and enjoyed fancy homes. Suddenly, I saw Jesus appear in the midst of it all. He was clothed in all white and walking in the opposite direction of those I'd been watching. I began to follow Him. He turned around and handed me three items: a nail, a ruler and a fig.

As leaders, we should be measuring spiritual growth within the body against the yardstick, the Word of God. We are to encourage fruitfulness in believers. We are to stabilize the people of God upon sound doctrine and not the promotion of prosperity without holiness. Fruitfulness and stability in the Word of God is the essence of true wealth. God once said to me that many are guilty of viewing success horizontally, focusing on what is seen in their immediate surroundings. But instead, we should view success vertically; it should be based upon our relationship with Him.

True wealth is forsaking all the world has to offer and going after the Giver of life. In Joshua 1:8, God

promises him good success if he remained obedient
to His Word. If there is good success then there is
bad success. Thus, we should not be quick to deem
someone righteous or anointed based upon where
they live or what they drive. Furthermore, the hard
truth is that many of us may never be rich in material

possessions. Hebrews 11:24–26 says:

> Aroused] by faith Moses, when he had grown
> to maturity and become great, refused to be
> called the son of Pharaoh's daughter, Because
> he preferred to share the oppression [suffer
> the hardships] and bear the shame of the
> people of God rather than to have the fleeting
> enjoyment of a sinful life. He considered the
> contempt and abuse and shame [borne for]
> the Christ (the Messiah Who was to come) to
> be greater wealth than all the treasures of
> Egypt, for he looked forward and away to the
> reward (recompense).

Mature Christians realize that all true wealth is in
God. It is not determined by what it is seen, but by
relationship with Jesus Christ. Many have forgotten
that, although Jesus had everything, He came to earth
with nothing—no material possessions. It is written,
He had nowhere to lay His head, yet He never lacked
anything. Everything He needed He created, because
He is the Word of God. Within Him is the power to
speak a word and it is done. That same power lies

within us. Acts 3:1–8 says:

> Now Peter and John were going up to the
> temple at the hour of prayer, the ninth hour
> (three o'clock in the afternoon), [When] a
> certain man crippled from his birth was being
> carried along, who was laid each day at that

162

gate of the temple [which is] called Beautiful, so that he might beg for charitable gifts from those who entered the temple. So when he saw Peter and John about to go into the temple, he asked them to give him a gift and Peter directed his gaze intently at him, and so did John, and said, Look at us! And [the man] paid attention to them, expecting that he was going to get something from them. But Peter said, Silver and gold (money) I do not have; but what I do have, that I give to you: in [the use of] the name of Jesus Christ of Nazareth, walk! Then he took hold of the man's right hand with a firm grip and raised him up. And at once his feet and ankle bones became strong and steady, and leaping forth he stood and began to walk, and he went into the temple with them, walking and leaping and praising God.

While the word *harlot* is used today to describe a promiscuous woman who sells what she has to get what she needs, interestingly, it was once used to refer to a certain kind of man. The word is first recorded in English in a work written around the 13th century, and meant "a man of no fixed occupation, vagabond, beggar," and soon afterwards meant "male lecher."[17]

So, lame from the womb, in the verse above, we see a harlot who sat daily at the entryway of the Beautiful Gate to beg for alms. Many walked by, saw him, empathized with him, and gave him money. However, his life drastically changed when true men of God walked his way. The wealth of power within the earthen vessels of Peter and John, spoke to the power lying dormant in the lame man. And that faithful day, he was given something money could not buy, the ability to walk.

In this season, the body of Christ is being crippled and thus their walk is hindered by messages promoted by spiritual harlots who limit God to financial prosperity alone. We are sitting around helpless, as common paupers when we have the Holy One living on the inside of us. We are hanging out outside of the gates of beautiful sanctuaries dressed in miniskirts and stilettos, with our hands extended looking for someone to fill them when God already fills our being. Day after day, we grow more and more lame because we are not properly instructed about walking in holiness and righteousness. It is time to become strong and steady in the Lord.

> So then, brace up *and* reinvigorate *and* set right your slackened *and* weakened *and* drooping hands and strengthen your feeble *and* palsied *and* tottering knees, and cut through *and* make firm *and* plain *and* smooth, straight paths for your feet [yes, make them safe and upright and happy paths that go in the right direction], so that the lame *and* halting [limbs] may not be put out of joint, but rather may be cured.

> —HEBREWS 12:12-13

I speak strength to the ankle bones and to the feet of those who have been weakened by falsity. Arise and walk. Rise up from false doctrine influenced by the spirit of mammon, rise up from sin and the love of the world, and walk. Walk in righteousness. Walk in love. Walk in purity, Walk in holiness, in the name of Jesus.

> Let your character or moral disposition be free from love of money [including greed, avarice, lust, and craving for earthly possessions] and be satisfied with your

> present [circumstances and with what you
> have].

—HEBREWS 13:5a

In a dream, I saw adults and children under the care of a leader. The leader took excellent care of the children, feeding them continuously. However, despite her efforts, they complained endlessly of their immense hunger. They were insatiable, unable to be filled. After dinner, they were taken to a theater which overflowed with the famous and the elite. The movie stars began to empty their drinks upon the heads of the children who admired them. In response, the children mimicked their actions by emptying their drinks upon the heads of each other.

The people in this dream reminded me of what I see in the time in which we live; the insatiable desire for gratification and the desire to be filled by the world instead of God. Mammon glamorizes the wealth of the world so that it is appealing to gain. God feeds and takes care of us while we turn to the world to be satisfied, finding it more filling. Mammon knows that once you have touched and tasted the wealth of the world in the natural, you will sell your soul spiritually to have it.

In these final days, God is going to drive out the false teachers. He is getting ready to turn over the tables of the moneychangers set up in His house. (See Mark 11:15–17.) A great separation is about to take place that will transition the true Christians to a place of unfathomable wealth and maturity in God.

> Come now, you rich [people], weep aloud and
> lament over the miseries (the woes) that are
> surely coming upon you. Your abundant

165

wealth has rotted and is ruined, and your [many] garments have become moth-eaten. Your gold and silver are completely rusted through, and their rust will be testimony against you and it will devour your flesh as if it were fire. You have heaped together treasure for the last days. [But] look! [Here are] the wages that you have withheld by fraud from the laborers who have reaped your fields, crying out [for vengeance]; and the cries of the harvesters have come to the ears of the Lord of hosts.

—JAMES 5:1–4

9

THE SPIRIT *of* OFFENSE

A brother offended is harder to be won over
than a strong city, and [their] contentions
separate them like the bars of a castle.

—PROVERBS 18:19

IN A DREAM, I watched a group of women of
different ethnicities and nationalities seated at a
dinner table inside of an upscale restaurant. I
could sense that the situation was highly
uncomfortable for them all. In fact, unable to bear the
awkward silence any longer, two women removed
themselves and sat at a different table. They did not
want to be seated amongst such a diverse array of
people. As the waitress circled the room, she did not
stop at either table to serve them. She was rude to
every woman in the restaurant. Suddenly, the women
of different cultural backgrounds had something in
common to discuss, the offensive behavior of their
negligent waitress.

We're imperfect human beings living in an
imperfect world, so offense is almost inevitable no
matter who we are. It is safe to assume that we have

all become offended at some point in our lives. Furthermore, I am certain that we have knowingly or unknowingly caused offense to someone else.

The spirit of offense is spreading, causing division throughout world, but particularly within the body of Christ. Within the walls of the sanctuary where God so graciously visits us, members often find themselves offended by the very ones called to lead them. Offense separates leaders from members, members from sanctuaries, and God from our lives.

John the Baptist was a great man of God, a true prophet, and was responsible for preparing the way of the Lord. He was given the amazing opportunity of baptizing God Himself. However, instead of getting glory on earth, he was captured and thrown into prison for speaking the truth. After realizing that Jesus was not coming to physically rescue him from prison, John the Baptist, in angst, sent a disciple to ask Jesus if He was the One and if so, why was he about to be decapitated. Jesus answered, "Blessed (happy, fortunate, and to be envied) is he who takes no offense at Me and finds no cause for stumbling in or through Me and is not hindered from seeing the Truth" (Matt. 11:6).

While John may have been offended, Jesus Himself had every excuse to become offended when John questioned His authority. He could have become offended when some did not believe He was the Son of God. He could have been offended when Judas betrayed Him, when Peter denied Him, when he was slapped in the face, when His beard was plucked, when He was mocked and a crown of thorns was pressed into His head. He could have become offended when He was nailed to the Cross for the very ones that crucified Him. But instead of becoming angry or trying to prove who He was, Jesus humbled Himself and interceded for us all, saying, "Father forgive them, for they know not what they do" (Luke 23:34).

> Let this same attitude and purpose and [humble] mind be in you which was in Christ Jesus: [Let Him be your example in humility:] Who, although being essentially one with God and in the form of God [possessing the fullness of the attributes which make God God], did not think this equality with God was a thing to be eagerly grasped or retained, But stripped Himself [of all privileges and rightful dignity], so as to assume the guise of a servant (slave), in that He became like men and was born a human being. And after He had appeared in human form, He abased and humbled Himself [still further] and carried His obedience to the extreme of death, even the death of the cross!
>
> —PHILIPPIANS 2:5–8

Satan makes every effort to cause circumstances or people to step into our path to offend us. It can be as simple as someone cutting us off in traffic or as damaging as a leader falling in sexual sin, scattering the flock of God. Why does Satan work overtime to line up offenses for us day after day? It would seem that offense is no big issue, especially when the dictionary says it is nothing more than "a lack of politeness, a failure to show regard for others and the wounding the feelings or others." Offense is a much deeper issue than hurt feelings alone because it opens the door to a host of other heinous spirits waiting for an opportunity to enter in and separate us from God. It has the possibility of manifesting as pure evil. James 1:14–15 says:

> But every person is tempted when he is drawn away, enticed and baited by his own evil desire (lust, passions). Then the evil desire, when it has conceived, gives birth to sin, and sin, when it is fully matured, brings forth death.

Offense is an evil seed that festers and grows into something that kills, possibly physically, but most certainly spiritually. From offense looms rebellion (witchcraft), bitterness, anger, hate and vengeance, which are all manifestations of the spirit of harlotry. The Word of God uses eighteen variations of the word *offense*. The Hebrew word *mikshol*[18] (stumbling block) means "an obstacle that can lead a person to stumble or to fall, or enticement [specifically an idol], scruple." Ezekiel 14:7–8 says:

> For anyone of the house of Israel or of the strangers who sojourn in Israel who separates himself from Me, taking his idols into his heart and putting the stumbling block of his iniquity and guilt before his face, and [yet] comes to the prophet to inquire for himself of Me, I the Lord will answer him Myself! And I will set My face against that [false worshiper] and will make him a sign and a byword, and I will cut him off from the midst of My people; and you shall know (understand and realize) that I am the Lord.

Offense blocks progression and it causes one to stumble and to fall. It entices and encourages individuals to avenge themselves, to rebel, and to harbor unforgiveness. It ruins lives and destinies by enticing or seducing the heart away from God.

SATAN USES FALSE LEADERS TO OFFEND

> Nevertheless, I have a few things against you: you have some people there who are clinging to the teaching of Balaam, who taught Balak to set a trap and a stumbling block before the sons of Israel, [to entice them] to eat food that had been sacrificed to idols and to practice lewdness [giving themselves up to sexual vice.
>
> —REVELATION 2:14

In speaking a word against the church, Jesus had a problem with Pergamon who allowed false teachings to hinder their walk. Once their hearts were opened up to the false teachings of Baal, stumbling blocks to progression and growth were inevitable.

In the New Testament, the Greek word *skandalon*[19] is translated as "one that stumbles or takes offense." *Skandalon* is where the English word *scandal* is derived. *Scandal* is defined as "a publicized incident that brings about disgrace or offends the moral sensibilities of society." The abnormally deceptive acts committed are called "scandals" because they challenge the standards which we consider to be "normal." We become offended by scandalous acts because they cause disgrace and shame. Typically scandals relate to the elite—those in high positions within government, entertainment industry, and even those regarded of high stature within the religious community. Satan has systematically placed stumbling blocks (false leaders) in pulpits across the nation. In

171

reviewing again the text from Samuel, we know that the sons of Eli were highly scandalous in nature. First Samuel 2:12–14, 22 says:

> Now the sons of Eli were sons of Belial; they knew not the LORD. And the priest's custom with the people was, that, when any man offered sacrifice, the priest's servant came, while the flesh was in seething, with a fleshhook of three teeth in his hand; And he struck it into the pan, or kettle, or caldron, or pot; all that the fleshhook brought up the priest took for himself. So they did in Shiloh unto all the Israelites that came thither.... Now Eli was very old, and he heard all that his sons did to all Israel and how they lay with the women who served at the door of the Tent of Meeting.

Masters of perversion, the sons of Eli's offenses included having sexual intercourse with the women of the church, fleecing the people of God, and defaming the offering of the Lord. Sadly, the presumptuous acts of Eli's sons are not foreign to the church.

The leaders' potential to lead the weak astray by their lifestyle is all too easy. Leaders must keep in mind that when a pulpit is mounted and words are spoken, the blood of those to whom they speak is on their hands. (See Ezekiel 33:6). Holiness is not mere words spoken from a pulpit; on the contrary, it is the ability to live by what was spoken once the pulpit has been dismounted. Simply put, are we practicing what we preach? In order for the body of Christ to produce fruit, they must first see the same fruit exhibited in the lives of those who profess to be their leaders. It is to be understood that God does not take lightly those who cause offense. For those who have become stumbling blocks to the people of God, a warning has been issued in Matthew 18:6–7.

> But whoever causes one of these little ones who believe in and acknowledge and cleave to Me to stumble and sin [that is, who entices him or hinders him in right conduct or thought], it would be better (more expedient and profitable or advantageous) for him to have a great millstone fastened around his neck and to be sunk in the depth of the sea. Woe to the world for such temptations to sin and influences to do wrong! It is necessary that temptations come, but woe to the person on whose account or by whom the temptation comes!

JESUS, ROCK OF OFFENSE

> For thus it stands in Scripture: Behold, I am laying in Zion a chosen (honored), precious chief Cornerstone, and he who believes in Him [who adheres to, trusts in, and relies on Him] shall never be disappointed or put to shame. To you then who believe (who adhere to, trust in, and rely on Him) is the preciousness; but for those who disbelieve [it is true], The [very] Stone which the builders rejected has become the main Cornerstone, And, A Stone that will cause stumbling and a Rock that will give [men] offense; they stumble because they disobey and disbelieve [God's] Word, as those [who reject Him] were destined (appointed) to do.

—1 PETER 2:6–8

Jesus was called a "rock of offense" a *skandalon*, however, Jesus does not entice anyone to sin. (See James 1:13.) Because of who He is—the Word of

God, the light, the truth, and the glory of God—He's considered an offense to the world. The message of Christ alone offends because His glorious light offends their darkness. Isaiah 8:13–14 says:

> The Lord of hosts—regard Him as holy and honor His holy name [by regarding Him as your only hope of safety], and let Him be your fear and let Him be your dread [lest you offend Him by your fear of man and distrust of Him]. And He shall be a sanctuary [a sacred and indestructible asylum to those who reverently fear and trust in Him]; but He shall be a Stone of stumbling and a Rock of offense to the houses of Israel, a trap and a snare to the inhabitants of Jerusalem.

In the presence of Jesus, the sins of the wicked leaders were manifested. They "stumbled" into sin because they refused to follow light. Jesus is the walking truth, the walking Word, and the Word is sharp and cuts deep. Acts 4:13, 17-18 says:

> Now when they saw the boldness and unfettered eloquence of Peter and John and perceived that they were unlearned and untrained in the schools [common men with no educational advantages], they marveled; and they recognized that they had been with Jesus....But in order that it may not spread further among the people and the nation, let us warn and forbid them with a stern threat to speak any more to anyone in this name [or about this Person]. [So] they summoned them and imperatively instructed them not to converse in any way or teach at all in or about the name of Jesus.

The "leaders" in the verses above explicitly warned Peter and John to desist from teaching in the name of Jesus. Thus, the spirit of offense is an intimidating spirit that frightens leaders into limiting the very name of Jesus. Many are submitting to the voices that whisper, "You can impress more people if you don't mention His name." Jesus Christ is the gospel. His works, His death, His resurrection, His cross, and His blood is what saved us all. How can the gospel of Christ be proclaimed without proclaiming the Christ of the gospel? Why is it the enemy's desire to have the name of Jesus eradicated? Philippians 2:7–11 says:

> But stripped Himself [of all privileges and rightful dignity], so as to assume the guise of a servant (slave), in that He became like men and was born a human being. And after He had appeared in human form, He abased and humbled Himself [still further] and carried His obedience to the extreme of death, even the death of the cross! Therefore [because He stooped so low] God has highly exalted Him and has freely bestowed on Him the name that is above every name, That in (at) the name of Jesus every knee should (must) bow, in heaven and on earth and under the earth, And every tongue [frankly and openly] confess and acknowledge that Jesus Christ is Lord, to the glory of God the Father.

You can chant to and call on Buddha, Muhammad, and other false gods all day long and nothing will happen. (See 1 Kings 18.) But at the name of Jesus something does. He has the name that is above every name. He has the name above sickness, the name above disease, the name above lack. When His name is mentioned minds are shifted, lives are changed, destinies are restored, and purposes are realigned. At the sound of His name, everything hindering a person's life must submit and bow. At the name of Jesus, the works of the enemy are destroyed.

As Christians, we are to remember that we will be considered offenses to the world without even trying. Operating according the desires of God is what sets us apart from the world. If we are walking in the true authority and power of God, we could merely walk inside of a room and people would become offended and convicted. Our lives should be open rebukes to the world, because it should not be us that is seen, but the Christ in us. Galatians 5:11 says:

> But, brethren, if I still preach circumcision [as some accuse me of doing, as necessary to salvation], why am I still suffering persecution? In that case the cross has ceased to be a stumbling block and is made meaningless (done away).

Here, the apostle Paul had been accused of preaching contrary the message of Christ. However, because of the persecutions he suffered, it is evident that he preached the truth. Apostle Paul's life would have been a lot easier had he proclaimed lies. Second Corinthians 11:24–28 recounts some of those persecutions:

> Five times I received from [the hands of] the Jews forty [lashes all] but one; Three times I have been beaten with rods; once I was stoned. Three times I have been aboard a ship wrecked at sea; a [whole] night and a day I have spent [adrift] on the deep; Many times on journeys, [exposed to] perils from rivers, perils from bandits, perils from [my own] nation, perils from the Gentiles, perils in the city, perils in the desert places, perils in the sea, perils from those posing as believers [but destitute of Christian knowledge and piety]; In

> toil and hardship, watching often [through
> sleepless nights], in hunger and thirst,
> frequently driven to fasting by want, in cold
> and exposure and lack of clothing. And
> besides those things that are without, there is
> the daily [inescapable pressure] of my care and
> anxiety for all the churches.

When preaching the Word of God as the Word of God, offense is inevitable. In fact, it is to be expected. Why? The world hates the Cross, because the Cross condemns the world. If we accept Jesus Christ then we must embrace the Cross, meaning we must die daily to the flesh and live lives of holiness. When we accept Jesus then our boast must be, "I have been crucified with Christ [in Him I have shared His crucifixion]; it is no longer I who live, but Christ (the Messiah) lives in me; and the life I now live in the body I live by faith in (by adherence to and reliance on and complete trust in) the Son of God, Who loved me and gave Himself up for me" (Gal. 2:20). The world cannot comprehend giving themselves up to allow Christ to live through them. They can't understand what Jesus did for us on the Cross, they consider it foolishness. So if the world loves us, then we should really evaluate what it is we are preaching and reevaluate whether or not it is Truth.

> For many will come in (on the strength of)
> My name [[appropriating the name which
> belongs to Me], saying, I am the Christ (the
> Messiah), and they will lead many astray. And
> you will hear of wars and rumors of wars; see
> that you are not frightened or troubled, for
> this must take place, but the end is not yet.
> For nation will rise against nation, and
> kingdom against kingdom, and there will be
> famines and earthquakes in place after place;

> All this is but the beginning [the early pains] of the [birth pangs [of the intolerable anguish]. Then they will hand you over to suffer affliction and tribulation and put you to death, and you will be hated by all nations for My name's sake. And then many will be offended and repelled and will begin to distrust and desert [Him Whom they ought to trust and obey] and will stumble and fall away and betray one another and pursue one another with hatred. And many false prophets will rise up and deceive and lead many into error. And the love of the great body of people will grow cold because of the multiplied lawlessness and iniquity.
>
> —MATTHEW 24:5–12

We have too many leaders attempting to attract the world for all of the wrong reasons. While some argue that, "We have to blend in with the world in order to attract the world," Jesus gave the mandate to go into the world and make disciples, not the other way around. (See Matthew 28:19.) I see nowhere in the Word of God that says we must be friends of the world in order to draw them. "You [are like] unfaithful wives [having illicit love affairs with the world and breaking your marriage vow to God]! Do you not know that being the world's friend is being God's enemy? So whoever chooses to be a friend of the world takes his stand as an enemy of God" (Jas 4:4).

The Word of God does not need any assistance from us. It is the truth and it is the way. Jesus was here before we breathed our first and at the end, He Is. John 12:32 says:

> And I, if and when I am lifted up from the
> earth [on the cross], will draw and attract all
> men [Gentiles as well as Jews] to Myself.

We must not be more concerned with full churches than we are with quality. If the motive behind "outreach" is not to draw others to God but to draw them to ourselves, then God is watching us. If the motive behind ministry is to gain notoriety, He knows. If the motive behind sermons is to sugarcoat sin and not pierce hearts into repentance, then God is bringing those false leaders down in the name of Jesus. When will the harvest of souls come? When Jesus Christ is lifted up! When will revival take place in our cities, churches, and hearts? When Jesus Christ is lifted up! John 11:9–10 says:

> Jesus answered, Are there not twelve hours in
> the day? Anyone who walks about in the
> daytime does not stumble, because he sees
> [by] the light of this world. But if anyone
> walks about in the night, he does stumble,
> because there is no light in him [the light is
> lacking to him].

Jesus is the light of the world and Jesus is the Word of God. If we do not walk in the illumination of the Word, we will fall into darkness every time. We will be easily swayed by every wind of doctrine that passes by. We will stumble because of a lack of knowledge. It is right when we cause others to become offended by the truth of the gospel. In that, we know we are being transformed more and more into the likeness of Christ—our Bridegroom.

PART II

THE
BREAKING
of
HARLOTRY

10

THE SPIRIT of ELIJAH

Behold, I will send you Elijah the prophet
before the great and terrible day of the Lord
comes. And he shall turn *and* reconcile the
hearts of the [estranged] fathers to the
[ungodly] children, and the hearts of the
[rebellious] children to [the piety of] their
fathers [a reconciliation produced by
repentance of the ungodly], lest I come and
smite the land with a curse *and* a ban of utter
destruction.

—MALACHI 4:5-6

A T LENGTH, WE have discussed the evils taking
place within the body of Christ. Because we
know the battle has already been won, we will
now discuss what I believe to be end-time
movements within the kingdom of God, through the
people of God, for such a time as this. It is especially
important to understand the significance of the role
of the spirit of Elijah in these final days. In the
natural, God used Elijah to conquer the spirit of
harlotry working through Queen Jezebel. Likewise,
God will dismantle the spirit of harlotry running

rampant by equipping believers to operate in the spirit of Elijah like never before.

While it is blatantly true that Satan has employed principalities and powers of wickedness in high places, he is no contender for our God. On our worst day, as anointed disciples of Christ, we have more power than the Enemy because "greater is He that is in us than he that is in the world" (1 John 4:4). The same power that raised Jesus Christ from the dead now lives in us. If we have this treasure living inside of these earthen vessels, then more Christians should arise as David and declare to all of hell, "You come to me with natural weapons, but I come in the name of the Lord of hosts, the God of the ranks of Israel." (See 1 Samuel 17:45.) Unlike Sampson, David was wise enough to realize that his sling itself had no power. He knew that the Spirit of God was the force behind the sling and the breath of God navigated the stone. "For though we walk (live) in the flesh, we are not carrying on our warfare according to the flesh and using human weapons. For the weapons of our warfare are not physical [weapons of flesh and blood] but they are mighty before God for the overthrow and destruction of strongholds" (1 Cor. 10:3-4).

Therefore, we must put down natural weapons and become aware of the power and the authority lying within us. We need not fight with weapons of iron and metal, because we come in the name of the One Who overcame the world. His name is Jesus Christ, and He is sharper than any two-edged sword. It is important to remember that for every problem, God already has a solution. For every flood, He has already set up a standard. The problem of apostasy in

Israel caused God to raise up a prophet by the name of Elijah. We read of him first in First Kings 17:1, which says:

> Elijah the Tishbite, of the temporary residents
> of Gilead, said to Ahab, As the Lord, the God
> of Israel, lives, before Whom I stand, there
> shall not be dew or rain these years but
> according to My word.

Initially, what I noticed about the text above was that there was no formal introduction of Elijah. With other prophets and apostles of the Old and New Testaments, there was often detailed information of their call, initial insecurities, and their assignments. For example, Scripture speaks of the reservations of both Moses and Jeremiah. It depicts the grandeur of Isaiah's call, how he witnessed the Lord high and lifted up. The apostle Paul was knocked off of his feet on the road to Damascus with an awesome vision of the Lord. Hosea's assignment involved marrying a harlot, and Ezekiel witnessed amazing visions of God and His heavenly host. So why was it that Elijah, such an awesome man of God, got no formal introduction? Why don't we hear anything of his call, his training, or why God chose him to become a vessel of such unbelievable miracles? What we do have is the verse above which says Elijah showed up with a word from God.

The word *inhabitants* in the original Hebrew is the same as "Tishbite." Some interpret the word *inhabitants* as meaning "stranger." The verse above could be read, "Elijah the Tishbite of Tishbi in Gilead" or "Elijah the stranger from among the strangers in Gilead." Elijah was seen as a stranger showing up when apostasy was at an all time high thanks to Jezebel and King Ahab.

In a dream, I watched a pastor on stage as he gave an illustrated message. Armed with weaponry and dressed in army fatigue, youth were standing on a stage beside him as he lined them up one by one. Like an airplane taking flight, the pastor ushered each youth off the stage and into a field. Among the youth were two young women. A male approached one of young women and asked her, "Are you second in command?" She looked at him and replied, "No, I'm first in command." Based upon appearance alone, the male in the dream made the assumption that he was speaking to an ordinary soldier. He had no idea he was speaking to a commander.

God is raising up an army of whom the world has never heard of. They will move in miracles, signs, and wonders much like the prophet Elijah. No one would suspect these to be commanders in the spirit. In fact, many will look at them and assume that they are too young or not "spiritually" qualified to handle the task at hand. Many will mistake their humility for spiritual infancy or timidity when in fact they have been digesting meat for quite some time. They have allowed God to elevate them and have not prematurely forced themselves upon platforms. They are full term and not preemies in the Spirit.

As said earlier, God often chooses the foolish and weak things of the world to confound the wise. (See 1 Corinthians 1:25–29.) God spoke to me once and said that He specializes in making the scavengers of the sea, the captains of the sea. Scavengers are the least of the least, the ones grazing slowly at the bottom of the ocean feeding on the leftovers, while the captains are seen as those who rule the sea. The least of the least are about to become the commanders in chief, the captains.

Another interesting aspect of the dream was that the youth were ushered off the stage as an airplane lifting off into flight. One moment they were being prepared and the next they were suited up and ready for battle. Just as Elijah appeared in the midst of turmoil with a Word from God; so will these end-time ministers of truth spring forth from what appears to be out of nowhere, in the midst of modern day apostasy. They have undergone undercover intense training sessions by the breath of the Lord, Himself.

It is true that God uses spiritual parents to help raise up new commanders in the earth, but there are times when God Himself trains His chosen. God used Paul to train Timothy, He used Moses to equip Joshua, He used Elijah to help Elisha, but who trained Elijah? I am in no way suggesting that this remnant will not be accountable to a local church or leadership. God is a God of decency and of order. (See 1 Corinthians 4:40.) Respect, accountability, and submission to leadership is imperative. These ministers will in no way be renegades or loose cannons in the body of Christ. There is enough of that as it is.

I am suggesting however, that we hear little about the call and training of Elijah because God used Elijah to implement something new in the earth. Elijah performed unprecedented, unheard of miracles. Nowhere in the Bible, before Elijah, had anyone proclaimed a drought or brought fire down from heaven. While mentoring and spiritual parentage is

187

still pertinent today, it is impossible for an individual to help one flow in a move of God that is foreign to them, because it has not been revealed to them. Some things that we will learn will result from being in the face of God and not in the face of man. In this hour, God is not allowing self imposed spiritual parents to stifle His young. There is no time to waste.

God has seen the spirit of harlotry loose in the world and influencing the body. As a response, He is raising up those who speak and it is done because God has spoken and they have not spoken by their own flesh. They will be considered strangers as Elijah, which is true. As Christians we are strangers to the world, but "friends" of God. (See 1 Peter 2:11.) Like Elijah they will need no introduction, the greater works of God will introduce them, the miracles of God will validate them. God Himself will ordain them. First Kings 18:15–22 says:

> Elijah said, As the Lord of hosts lives, before Whom I stand, I will surely show myself to Ahab today. So Obadiah went to meet Ahab and told him, and Ahab went to meet Elijah. Therefore send and gather to me all Israel at Mount Carmel, and the 450 prophets of Baal and the 400 prophets of [the goddess] Asherah, who eat at [Queen] Jezebel's table. So Ahab sent to all the Israelites and assembled the prophets at Mount Carmel. Elijah came near to all the people and said, How long will you halt and limp between two opinions? If the Lord is God, follow Him! But if Baal, then follow him. And the people did not answer him a word. Then Elijah said to the people, I, I only, remain a prophet of the Lord, but Baal's prophets are 450 men.

188

There was a challenge of the gods that day much like the invisible war taking place between the Enemy and us today. Elijah "showed" himself to Ahab. The word *show* means "to expose or reveal the true character or nature of." It can also mean "a performance and public spectacle." When Elijah said that he would, "show" himself, I believe he showed all that God had been revealing to him in secret. Everything God had placed in his belly were about to manifest before the eyes of his enemies. When he said that he would show himself, God planned to reveal His power through Elijah, putting an end to Jezebel's magic show. The time is near when the body will not be swayed by stage performances; there is enough of that in Hollywood. The spirit of Elijah will counteract the spirit of Jezebel in these final hours with a showdown.

In a dream, I witnessed a family who was grieving the loss of a loved one. The deceased was a mother and a wife. After the funeral, there was a parade that was allegedly given in her honor. However, I sensed that those leading the parade were not concerned about celebrating the woman's life at all. Their only desire was to be seen and to be the center of attention. The husband of the deceased watched those leading the parade and said, "They do not belong there; we should be there in their place."

A parade is defined as "show" or "performance." In this dream, God is saying that His people are dying spiritual deaths and those in leadership are only concerned about performances and appearances. However, there is about to be a divine shift and those who are merely hiding behind false pretenses will be shown up by those who God truly ordained "to be in their place." No longer will the world have to hear about who God was, they are about to see who He is because Jesus has already disarmed principalities and powers, making a public spectacle of the enemy. (See 2 Colossians 2:15.)

Everything Elijah did was done "in the name of the Lord." The leaders who God will use in these final days will make no mistake of claiming God's glory for themselves. Leaders in high places have allowed people to worship them and not the God who sent them. In many instances, no effort of correction has been implemented to cause the members to cease from the glorification of man. God has a remedy, and it is to strip every ounce of glory they have accessed illegally. They will be shifted from high places and back to the valley. He has said in His Word, "No flesh should glory in [My] presence." (See 1 Corinthians 1:29, NKJV.)

In another dream, I watched an ill man sitting in the middle of a church in a wheel chair. As he sat in terrible pain, leaders walked around his wheelchair as if he didn't exist. Then I heard the word *farce*, which may be used interchangeably with "parade" or "charade." The sick and wounded come to the house of God to be set free, healed, and delivered. However, they are being ignored. The house of God is being transformed into a house of charades. Many parade around in "robes of righteousness" with hearts that are divided; they parade around upon self erected platforms and throw around self given titles. It is now popular to have a title in front of the name. Many claim to be God's prophet, apostle, teacher, pastor, or evangelist because it sounds good. Question, if there are so many fivefold ministers throughout the world, why are so many bodies being buried, why is cancer claiming more and more lives by the minute, why are there so many missing limbs on natural bodies and in the body of Christ? As many alleged leaders as there are in the body, we should have the devil on the run because as we see in 1 Kings 18 it only took one true prophet of God to take down 450 of the false.

God told me once, "My children grow weary from hearing about miracles that happened back in the day." As spiritual beings we are attracted to spiritual things. As a response to this craving, the world seeks out psychics while the church attempts to impress them with speech and eloquence. The world does not want to hear about how Jesus rebuked death and disease. They want to see us Spirit-filled believers *do* it. It was Jesus Himself who said, "Greater works shall you do." My question to the body as a whole, but particularity in the United States is, where are those greater works? Where are those who call fire down from heaven? Where are those who herald, "thus says the Lord," and it actually happens? Where are the Spirit-filled believers who curse disease and raise the dead?

As Christians, we are under a microscope. The world is ready to find any reason to deny Christ, and what greater reason is there for them to mock us than for false ministers, with no power, to prophesy lies in the name of Jesus. The name of God is blasphemed among the Gentiles because of lying teachers. (See Romans 2:24.) Jeremiah 23:25–27 says:

> I have heard what the prophets have said who prophesy lies in My name, saying, I have dreamed, I have dreamed [visions on my bed at night]. [How long shall this state of things

continue?] How long yet shall it be in the minds of the prophets who prophesy falsehood, even the prophets of the deceit of their own hearts, who think that they can cause My people to forget My name by their dreams which every man tells to his neighbor, just as their fathers forgot My name because of Baal?

THE TRUE VOICE OF GOD

There he came to a cave and lodged in it; and behold, the word of the Lord came to him, and He said to him, What are you doing here, Elijah? He replied, I have been very jealous for the Lord God of hosts; for the Israelites have forsaken Your covenant, thrown down Your altars, and killed Your prophets with the sword. And I, I only, am left; and they seek my life, to take it away. And He said, Go out and stand on the mount before the Lord. And behold, the Lord passed by, and a great and strong wind rent the mountains and broke in pieces the rocks before the Lord, but the Lord was not in the wind; and after the wind an earthquake, but the Lord was not in the earthquake; And after the earthquake a fire, but the Lord was not in the fire; and after the fire [a sound of gentle stillness and] a still, small voice.

—1 KINGS 19:9–12

God commanded Elijah to stand on the mountain, and after the strong wind tore the mountains into pieces before the Lord, Elijah soon discovered that God was not in the wind. This is to say that while false prophets may perform superficial tricks and fleeting magic shows, what God does is not in the wind. He is not here one day and gone the next. Likewise, we are not to be blown away on every

192

wind of false doctrine. (See Ephesians 4:14.) After the wind, an earthquake came but God wasn't in the earthquake either. The dictionary defines earthquake as "a sudden movement in the earth resulting from underground movement." Earthquakes cause extensive damage in the earth realm and have the potential to destroy possessions and claim the lives of thousands at a time.

In recent years, there have been a lot of sudden movements that claim to have originated with God. They are moving heavily in the spirit of Babylon, which originated from the underground. Like natural earthquakes, spiritual earthquakes (false, demonic movements) are created to destroy all those that walk the face of the earth who truly serve God. They are created to cause chaos in the spiritual realm but Gamaliel said it best when he said, "For if this doctrine or purpose or undertaking or movement is of human origin, it will fail (be overthrown and come to nothing)." (See Acts 5:38.) If God is not in it, it will not stand.

After the earthquake, there was a fire, but God was not in that fire. As discussed earlier, seemingly every day ministries arise claiming to operate in the "fire" of God. Fires initiated without God are equivalent to "strange fires." Many are professing to have supernatural experiences but they originated from the underworld and they are in covenant with Babylon. Those professing to be on fire for the Lord, but have no evidence of power, will be put out by the Lord Himself in this hour.

Finally, we see that God spoke to Elijah in a "still small voice." Even though Elijah became intimidated by Jezebel's threats and ran, he learned to hear the voice of the Lord in a different way. How did Elijah know that God was not in the wind, earthquake, or the fire? It was simply because he knew and discerned the voice of God. The lack of discernment has left the door open and flies have flown in causing a stench throughout the house of God. We have begun to welcome strange fires and demonic earthquakes. We have embraced temporal sideshow tricks that came from the pits of hell. We lack discernment and cannot distinguish between a move of God and a magic show from the enemy. We are not tuned in to the still small voice of God as we should be. However, in the midst of onslaught from the Enemy, God is raising up those who remain steadfast, those who are sensitive to His voice and His beckon. We have been playing the harlot in a theater production called *Deception* but the curtains are finally about to close. First Kings 19:16–18 continues:

> And anoint Jehu son of Nimshi to be king over Israel, and anoint Elisha son of Shaphat of Abel-meholah to be prophet in your place. And him who escapes from the sword of Hazael Jehu shall slay, and him who escapes the sword of Jehu Elisha shall slay. Yet I will leave Myself 7,000 in Israel, all the knees that have not bowed to Baal and every mouth that has not kissed him.

In a vision, I saw the Lord wrap His arms around a belly; inside of the belly was a blazing fire. Where was this remnant of prophets hiding that even the prophet Elijah did not know?

There is a remnant of leaders that God has kept for Himself. He has protected His word within them, set them on high, and hidden them under the shadow of His wings because they have known His name.

194

(See Psalm 91:14.) He has kept them from being slain by the evils of this world for such a time as this. He has those whom He is willing to show Himself mightily to because they have already become well acquainted with His face.

11

THE ANOINTING *of* JEHU

And anoint Jehu son of Nimshi to be king
over Israel, and anoint Elisha son of Shaphat
of Abel-meholah to be prophet in your place.
And him who escapes from the sword of
Hazael Jehu shall slay, and him who escapes
the sword of Jehu Elisha shall slay.

—1 KINGS 19:16–17

AS WE CONTINUE exploring the showdown
between Elijah and Jezebel, there is one point
that is often missed, the role that Jehu played.
What's most-often highlighted is the battle between
Elijah and Jezebel. However, it was at the hand of
Jehu, by the Spirit of God that Jezebel and the
household of Ahab was finally overthrown. Jehu, the
son of Jehoshaphat and grandson of Nimshi, was
initially a bodyguard for Ahab and thus Jehu had the
opportunity to witness first-hand, the sinister deeds of
his employer. He had possibly watched as Ahab
schemed to steal land that rightfully belonged to
Naboth. Undoubtedly, he had seen the battle that
took place between Elijah and Ahab in the vineyard.

Because of his position and ungodly connections, it would appear as though Jehu was an unlikely candidate to be anointed and used by God. But when God gets ready to anoint a specific person for a specific task, He does not care about past or current connections, position, or posture. He is looking for willing vessels with a "yes," not only upon their lips, but in their hearts. When He calls, we have a responsibility to answer. It is evident that Jehu answered and said yes. God is calling the least likely candidates to be His anointed vessels of deliverance. He is literally transforming what the world views as the weak and debased into instruments of mass destruction, which leads me to the first characteristic of the Jehu anointing.

1. SLAYS

> And him who escapes from the sword of Hazael Jehu shall slay…

Jehu's anointing was unusual but effective. The word *slay* is defined as "to kill intentionally and with premeditation, to cause to die; put to death, to knowingly annihilate." The anointing that God placed upon Jehu was one that intentionally put to death those in opposition to Him. In this case, Jehu had a planned, premeditated assignment of annihilating the household of Ahab, those who sought to silence the voice of the true prophets of God. Hosea 6:5 says:

> Therefore have I hewn down and smitten them by means of the prophets; I have slain them by the words of My mouth; My judgments [pronounced upon them by you prophets] are like light that goes forth.

Second Thessalonians 2:8 says:

> And then the lawless one (the antichrist) will
> be revealed and the Lord Jesus will slay him
> with the breath of His mouth and bring him
> to an end by His appearing at His coming.

God is about to release an army of leaders with
this "slayer" anointing. This army will have but one
objective and that is to seek out the opposing forces
of God and slay everything that is unlike Him. They
will not use physical swords as Jehu, they will wield
the sword of the Spirit.

> For the Word that God speaks is alive and full
> of power [making it active, operative,
> energizing, and effective]; it is sharper than
> any two-edged sword, penetrating to the
> dividing line of the breath of life (soul) and
> [the immortal] spirit, and of joints and
> marrow [of the deepest parts of our nature],
> exposing and sifting and analyzing and
> judging the very thoughts and purposes of the
> heart.
>
> —HEBREWS 4:12

This slayer anointing will be enforced by God as
His Word is proclaimed, uncompromised and
unadulterated. Using the sword of truth they will
annihilate all that is false in their midst. The truth will
literally slay the darkness of false doctrine and sin that
has been erected inside of the hearts of the
multitudes. Those anointed with the Jehu anointing
will have ministries similar to that of the prophet
Jeremiah because God has truly placed His Word into
their mouths. While others have feasted upon words
of man, God has commanded them to ruminate upon
His Word. Why? Out of the abundance of the heart

the mouth speaks. (See Luke 6:45.) Popularity will not be their lot; many will hate them. They will become acquainted with mocking and clamoring. While famous preachers across the world gain notoriety and applause, these individuals will often walk in embarrassment, because much like the apostle Paul, their revelation will be great. Their one sole purpose will be to proclaim the Word of God as it is given and as it is written. Second Kings 9:1–2 continues:

> And Elisha the prophet called one of the sons of the prophets and said to him, Gird up your loins, take this flask of oil in your hand, and go to Ramoth-gilead. When you arrive, look there for Jehu son of Jehoshaphat son of Nimshi; and go in and have him arise from among his brethren and lead him to an inner chamber.

Jehu was called to arise from among his brethren, from the known. Often those who are set apart must stand alone. When God anoints us for a specific task, the time will come when we must separate ourselves from circumstances, people, places, and things that have become familiar and comfortable. The time will come when we must arise from complacency and normalcy to attain the greatness that God has spoken over our lives and placed within our bellies. Unfortunately, most fail to realize the importance of separation. Many whom God chose have reverted to their old habits. Instead of rising up, they have taken a back seat in the presence of the world.

After arising Jehu was called into the "inner chamber." The inner chamber is symbolic of prayer and spending time with God. As the anointed of God we are called to a higher place. We are called to spend time in the Lord and with the Lord. It is by prayer that the will of God can be done on earth as it is in heaven. It is required of anyone who seeks to operate in the anointing of God, but sadly many fall short.

Matthew 6:1–8 says:

> And when ye pray, ye shall not be as the hypocrites: for they love to stand and pray in the synagogues and in the corners of the streets, that they may be seen of men. Verily I say unto you, They have received their reward. But thou, when thou prayest, enter into thine inner chamber, and having shut thy door, pray to thy Father which is in secret, and thy Father which seeth in secret shall recompense thee. And in praying use not vain repetitions, as the Gentiles do: for they think that they shall be heard for their much speaking. Be not therefore like unto them: for your Father knoweth what things ye have need of, before ye ask him.
>
> —ERV(English Revised Version)

In the text above, Jesus discusses the hypocrites who professed to know the Lord but their only desire was to be seen by men. They were liars who repeated vain repetitions of prayer only to be heard.

It is amazing to me how so many stand in the house of the Lord and boast lies. A lie is not only something that we speak with our mouths, but also how we live. Lifestyle liars can be found in choir stands, usher boards, leadership, as well as the pulpit. Monday through Saturday they look like, smell like, and sound like the world, but on Sunday they dress in priestly garments. We had better make sure that we have not likened ourselves to those the Lord speaks of in Matthew 8:21; those who cast out demons, build huge ministries, and prophesy but the Lord does not know them. Many who have served out of the wrong spirit will hear the Lord say "Depart from me. I know you not," because all of their works were vain, empty, and worthless.

2. SWIFT

> Then take the cruse of oil and pour it on his head and say, Thus says the Lord: I have anointed you king over Israel. Then open the door and flee; do not tarry. So the young man, the young prophet, went to Ramoth-gilead. And when he came, the captains of the army were sitting outside; and he said, I have a message for you, O captain. Jehu said, To which of us? And he said, To you, O captain. And Jehu arose, and they went into the house. And the prophet poured the oil on Jehu's head and said to him, Thus says the Lord, the God of Israel: I have anointed you king over the people of the Lord, even over Israel....And he opened the door and fled.
>
> —2 KINGS 9:3–6, 10b

The young prophet was obedient to what the prophet Elisha had instructed him to do. He anointed Jehu with a flask of oil, pouring it upon his head, then fled because he was told "not to tarry." So we see a young man acting rather strangely, literally running away after he anointed Jehu.

God has various ways of helping our minds to conceive heavenly information. The use of prophetic actions is one of those ways. I believe the young man running out of the door swiftly was a prophetic action indicating the anointing that would come upon Jehu, was a swift anointing that did not waste time. Samuel anointed David in a similar fashion to that of Jehu in that he was anointed with a flask. The notable difference between the two occasions is that while David would not act as king for several years, Jehu reigned almost immediately. This impels me to believe that the anointing of Jehu is the anointing of a "swift work." It causes one to move swiftly to get what God has spoken completed.

I had a vision of a train traveling at top speed. Seated inside of the train were thousands of people. I saw a man standing ahead on the track as the train quickly approached. He had every opportunity to step off of the train track before it arrived, yet he did not. I heard the Lord say, "This is the hour that I do a quick work and anything that gets in the way of what I am doing will be annihilated." We know that a train will not stop to save the life of one individual because it would put the thousands who are already on the train in jeopardy. There is a great urgency in the Spirit and those who attempt to delay or frustrate what God is doing, will be utterly destroyed in the process. Also, those who think that they are irreplaceable and have begun to stray will be replaced quickly in this season by those who are passionate and full of holy zeal.

3. EVIDENT AND POTENT

When Jehu came out to the servants of his master, one said to him, Is all well? Why did this mad fellow come to you? And he said to them, You know that class of man and what he would say. And they said, That is false; tell us now. And he said, Thus and thus he spoke to me, saying, Thus says the Lord: I have anointed you king over Israel. Then they

203

> hastily took every man his garment and put it
> [for a cushion] under Jehu on the top of the
> [outside] stairs, and blew with trumpets,
> saying, Jehu is king!

—2 KINGS 9:11–13

The Jehu anointing is not only one that slays and one that is swift, but it is also an anointing that is evident and potent. Jehu merely spoke what God had spoken to him and the soldiers once loyal to Ahab believed Jehu and switched sides. The soldiers removed their garments which was symbolic of their old beliefs and alliances. When you are truly anointed of God, there is no need for self-promotion. Neither is there need to add to what God has already spoken. All we have to do is speak the Word of God and blinded eyes will be opened, chains will be removed, bodies will be healed, and lives converted. Second Kings 9:17–20 says:

> A watchman on the tower in Jezreel spied the
> company of Jehu as he came, and said, I see a
> company. And Joram said, Send a horseman
> to meet them and have him ask, Do you come
> in peace? So one on horseback went to meet
> him and said, Thus says the king: Is it peace?
> And Jehu said, What have you to do with
> peace? Rein in behind me. And the watchman
> reported, The messenger came to them, but
> he does not return. Then Joram sent out a
> second man on horseback, who came to them
> and said, Thus says the king: Is it peace? Jehu
> replied, What have you to do with peace? Ride
> behind me. And the watchman reported, He
> came to them, but does not return; also the
> driving is like the driving of Jehu son of
> Nimshi, for he drives furiously.

204

Jehu wasted no time. The anointing was upon him, and it caused him to take swift, immediate action. The slaying assignment in his belly was as a consuming fire. It would either consume him for not completing it or consume the evil around him. Jehu chose the latter.

The soldiers approaching Jehu asked, "Are you coming in peace?" He simply answered, "What do you know about peace? Fall behind me." On two instances neither guard put up a fight but immediately fell behind him. Second Kings 9:21–26 says:

> Joram said, Make ready. When his chariot was made ready, Joram king of Israel and Ahaziah king of Judah When Joram saw Jehu, he said, is it peace, Jehu? And he answered, How can peace exist as long as the fornications of your mother Jezebel and her witchcrafts are so many? Then Joram reined about and fled, and he said to Ahaziah, Treachery, Ahaziah! But Jehu drew his bow with his full strength and shot Joram between his shoulders; and the arrow went out through his heart, and he sank down in his chariot. Then said Jehu to Bidkar his captain, Take [Joram] up and cast him in the plot of Naboth the Jezreelite's field; for remember how, when I and you rode together after Ahab his father, the Lord uttered this prophecy against him: As surely as I saw yesterday the blood of Naboth and the blood of his sons, says the Lord, I will repay you on this plot of ground, says the Lord. Now therefore, take and cast Joram into the plot of ground [of Naboth], as the word of the Lord said.

When Joram realized Jehu did not come in peace and that his servants had turned on him, he began to prepare for battle—to no avail, however. Jehu took his bow and arrow and shot Joram between the shoulders and through his heart. The anointing of Jehu flows heavily in turning the hearts of men; those anointed as Jehu will take the Word of God and penetrate the hearts of men. (See Hebrews 4:12.) After killing Joram, Jehu commanded the soldiers to cast his body on the very land that was stolen from Naboth. Proverbs 9:17–18 says:

> Stolen waters (pleasures) are sweet [because they are forbidden]; and bread eaten in secret is pleasant. But he knows not that the shades of the dead are there [specters haunting the scene of past transgressions], and that her invited guests are [already sunk] in the depths of Sheol (the lower world, Hades, the place of the dead).

Likewise, the stolen pleasures of this world in which some deem important enough to deny the truth, will lead to their demise. Looking further, we see that Jehu continues to slay the house of Ahab and prophecy is fulfilled. Second Kings 9:29–33 reads:

> In the eleventh year of Joram son of Ahab, Ahaziah's reign over Judah began. Now when Jehu came to Jezreel, Jezebel heard of it, and she painted her eyes and beautified her head and looked out of [an upper] window. And as Jehu entered in at the gate, she said, [Have you come in] peace, you Zimri, who slew his master? Jehu lifted up his face to the window and said, Who is on my side? Who? And two or three eunuchs looked out at him. And he said, Throw her down! So they threw her down, and some of her blood splattered on

the wall and on the horses, and he drove over
her.

A much older Jezebel heard Jehu approaching and
began to dress herself in her harlotrous "priestly
garments," placed makeup upon her eyelids, and tied
up her hair. It would appear as though Jezebel was
attempting to seduce Jehu into sparing her life.
However, I believe her makeup and attire was
representative of her undying devotion to Baal.
Dressed in her war paint and pagan garments, she
displayed her prideful nature and unrepentant heart.
(See Revelation 2:21.)

Her reasoning for dressing herself is unknown,
but one thing was certain, Jehu, equipped with the
slayer anointing and the Word of God in his heart,
was not falling for the subtle devices of Satan. Jezebel
questioned Jehu, but he wasted no time answering her
because he knew who it was he was dealing with and
chose not to flirt with death. Likewise, we can't waste
time playing the harlot with Jezebel. We don't have
the luxury of continuously talking about the issues at
hand. We must move and act. We must remain
focused and dedicated to the task at hand and not
become enticed away by the seductive schemes of
Satan.

Wasting not a moment of time, Jehu lifted up his
face and spoke directly to Jezebel's eunuchs saying,
"Who is on my side?" The term *eunuch* usually refers
to those castrated (without their consent) in order to
perform a specific social function. They were
considered weak because missing male reproductive
organs, they were unable to produce. But not only
were they unproductive, they couldn't even perform.
Because of this, eunuchs were often overlooked. They

were seen but not seen, heard but not listened to. This is how the spirit of Jezebel operates today. It intimidates the weak-minded of the church—the ones who don't have the ability to produce, the ones who are viewed as "spiritual nobodies" in God. It targets the overlooked because Satan knows what many of us as "mature" believers choose to overlook, God uses the unlikely. Because spiritual eunuchs have a desire to be noticed, Jezebel can easily entice them into her lair by showing them attention needed from their leaders. First Corinthians 1:27–28 says:

> [No] for God selected (deliberately chose) what in the world is foolish to put the wise to shame, and what the world calls weak to put the strong to shame. And God also selected (deliberately chose) what in the world is lowborn and insignificant and branded and treated with contempt, even the things that are nothing, that He might depose and bring to nothing the things that are.

God is vindicating the lost by His Spirit. He is calling them into their true purpose. The substance of the spiritual eunuchs of this world has been seen by Him and He will use them to help destroy the yoke of the spirit of Jezebel in this season.

> And he said, Throw her down! So they threw her down, and some of her blood splattered on the wall and on the horses, and he drove over her.
>
> —2 KINGS 9:33

The eunuchs quickly submitted to the anointing upon Jehu and threw Jezebel from the window. As followers of Christ operating in the anointing, there will be times when we don't have to speak, we don't have to yell; the anointing of God will speak for us. We must remember when Jesus healed and performed miracles, He'd simply say, "Talitha Cumi" or "Rise and walk." (See Mark 5:41.) Second Kings 9:35–37 continues:

> They went to bury her, but they found nothing left of her except the skull, feet, and palms of her hands. They came again and told Jehu. He said, This is the word of the Lord which He spoke by His servant Elijah the Tishbite, In the portion of Jezreel shall dogs eat the flesh of Jezebel. The corpse of Jezebel shall be like dung upon the face of the field in the portion of Jezreel, so that they shall not say, this is Jezebel.

In this portion of Scripture, the prophecy of Elijah is fulfilled. Jezebel was trampled by horses until nothing remained of her but her skull, feet, and the palms of her hands. The human skull, as we know, houses the brain, which is the center of higher-order thinking, learning, and memory. The brain monitors, regulates, and controls bodily actions and functions. It is responsible for the body's balance, posture, and the coordination of movement. Romans 8:5–8 reads:

> For those who are according to the flesh and are controlled by its unholy desires set their minds on and pursue those things which gratify the flesh, but those who are according to the Spirit and are controlled by the desires of the Spirit set their minds on and seek those things which gratify the [Holy] Spirit. Now the mind of the flesh [which is sense and reason without the Holy Spirit] is death [death

that comprises all the miseries arising from sin, both here and hereafter]. But the mind of the [Holy] Spirit is life and [soul] peace [both now and forever]. [That is] because the mind of the flesh [with its carnal thoughts and purposes] is hostile to God, for it does not submit itself to God's Law; indeed it cannot. So then those who are living the life of the flesh [catering to the appetites and impulses of their carnal nature] cannot please or satisfy God, or be acceptable to Him.

God is destroying the worldly mind-sets that throw off the balance and the posture of the body of Christ and He is regulating the body by His Spirit. The sharpness of His Word will be spoken in the appropriate seasons and will consume the sin and iniquity in the lives of the listeners. The fact that Jezebel's skull remained after her death, was representative of the fact that her ideas and beliefs were worthless without having a body to control. Jezebel's hands represented her evil deeds and her feet, the way she walked. Everything she put her hands to was evil and her feet followed the evil dictates of her unrepentant, vile heart.

The day is coming that the spirit of Jezebel will be brought down by the spirit of Jehu enforced by the Word of God. Those who walk according to the dictates of the flesh, put their hands to evil, and have allowed their wicked mind-sets to dominate their steps, will be consumed by their own evil. We must not give harlotry a body to control. If we refuse the truth, our souls will be consumed by the fire of hell. But if we accept the truth, our fleshly desires will be consumed, granting us eternal life. (See Matthew 25:46.)

12

THE SPIRIT *of* GLORY

> In the beginning God (prepared, formed,
> fashioned, and) created the heavens and the
> earth. The earth was without form and an
> empty waste, and darkness was upon the face
> of the very great deep. The Spirit of God was
> moving (hovering, brooding) over the face of
> the waters. And God said, Let there be light;
> and there was light. And God saw that the
> light was good (suitable, pleasant) and He
> approved it; and God separated the light from
> the darkness.
>
> —GENESIS 1:1–4

FROM THE VERY beginning, the importance of
separating light from darkness is made evident
by the Lord. Throughout the Word of God, we
find that light is associated with Christ and His
followers. First Thessalonians 5:5 says, "For you are
all sons of light and sons of the day; we do not belong
either to the night or to darkness." Darkness, which is
attributed to Satan and his works is defined as "the
absence of light." Thus, darkness has no meaning on

its own and without light, it has no purpose. John 1:1–5, 10 says:

> In the beginning [before all time] was the Word (Christ), and the Word was with God, and the Word was God Himself. He was present originally with God. All things were made and came into existence through Him; and without Him was not even one thing made that has come into being. In Him was Life, and the Life was the Light of men. And the Light shines on in the darkness, for the darkness has never overpowered it [put it out or absorbed it or appropriated it, and is unreceptive to it]....There it was—the true Light [was then] coming into the world [the genuine, perfect, steadfast Light] that illumines every person. He came into the world, and though the world was made through Him, the world did not recognize Him [did not know Him].

The Word of God, Jesus Christ, came as light shining in the midst of darkness, yet the world did not know Him. Much like then, we live in a time where many do not know the Lord. As discussed earlier, while most claim to know Him, they merely know of His existence. Statistics reveal that there is not an absence of professing Christians; quite the contrary, there is an abundance. However, there is an absence of true Christians, those who whole-heartedly serve the Lord, walking in His divine light.

Satan has an end-time agenda of drawing as many as possible away from the truth and toward the false light emanating. He exists to destroy the children of light. Since the beginning with Adam and Eve, it has been his sole purpose to introduce man to darkness, marketing it as light, for he masquerades as an angel of light. (See 2 Corinthians 11:14.) Genesis 3:6–7 says:

> And when the woman saw that the tree was good (suitable, pleasant) for food and that it was delightful to look at, and a tree to be desired in order to make one wise, she took of its fruit and ate; and she gave some also to her husband, and he ate. Then the eyes of them both were opened, and they knew that they were naked; and they sewed fig leaves together and made themselves apronlike girdle.

Prior to the fall, Adam and Eve were in the presence of the Lord continually. When they followed the dark counsel of the enemy, their eyes were opened to darkness. Rejecting God, they instantly became desensitized to Him and sensitized to the sin and spiritual pollution of the world. Suddenly they were naked, because where the glory of the Lord is, there is also an illumination of our own filthiness as human beings.

There are two Hebrew words used for the word *naked* in Genesis 2 and 3. In Genesis 2:25, prior to the Fall, the Hebrew word *arom*[20] which means "partially naked," is used. It is interesting to note that after the Fall in Genesis 3:7, Adam and Eve were *erom*[21], which means "totally naked." How is it that initially they were only partially naked and after the Fall they were totally naked? I believe it was because Adam and Eve were not physically naked to begin with. They were actually covered in a mantle of light or *kabod*[22] (glory), which was a result of being in the presence of God constantly. This can be likened to Moses when he stood in the presence of Lord and afterwards had to veil his face because it illuminated so brightly. *Glory* in the Hebrew is *kabod* which means "heavy or weighty." Adam and Even were clothed in a heavy, weighty mantle of the glory of God, their bodies were illuminated by His glory. It was only when the Enemy slipped in exposing them to the knowledge of good and evil, that they were stripped of their covering.

As a result of their disobedience, they became totally naked and exposed. For us as Christians, darkness is not only representative of worldly darkness but also spiritual darkness, a lack of Godly wisdom. Because many have opened themselves up to dark counsel, they have shut the door to the voice of God. Many have been stripped bare and are spiritually naked. Romans 1:20-23 says:

> For ever since the creation of the world His invisible nature and attributes, that is, His eternal power and divinity, have been made intelligible and clearly discernible in and through the things that have been made (His handiworks). So [men] are without excuse [altogether without any defense or justification], because when they knew and recognized Him as God, they did not honor and glorify Him as God or give Him thanks. But instead they became futile and godless in their thinking [with vain imaginings, foolish reasoning, and stupid speculations] and their senseless minds were darkened. Claiming to be wise, they became fools [professing to be smart, they made simpletons of themselves]. And by them the glory and majesty and excellence of the immortal God were exchanged for and represented by images, resembling mortal man and birds and beasts and reptiles.

Genesis 3:7 says that Adam and Eve created aprons to cover their nakedness. The Hebrew word for "apron" in this text is *chagorah*. This is translated as "something which to gird about, a loin covering, belt, armor." This word is also used in Ephesians 6:14 where we are instructed to "gird our loins with the belt of truth." However, instead of accepting the truth that God had given to them, Adam and Eve decided to gird their loins with the darkness of the enemy. They exchanged their mantle of glory for the works of their own hands, an apron constructed of leaves, which was temporal. Second Corinthians 4:4–6 reads:

> For the god of this world has blinded the unbelievers' minds [that they should not discern the truth], preventing them from seeing the illuminating light of the Gospel of the glory of Christ (the Messiah), Who is the Image and Likeness of God. For what we preach is not ourselves but Jesus Christ as Lord, and ourselves [merely] as your servants (slaves) for Jesus' sake. For God Who said, Let light shine out of darkness, has shone in our hearts so as [to beam forth] the Light for the illumination of the knowledge of the majesty and glory of God [as it is manifest in the Person and is revealed] in the face of Jesus Christ (the Messiah).

There is a false light illuminating in the world today in the form of dark knowledge that began in the underworld. This false light is attempting to overshadow the truth. This is why the enemy takes the Word of God and distorts it, creating appealing lies. Many influential leaders follow the false light in exchange for man-made glory. However, we must directly and forcefully oppose the works of darkness because we were created to manifest the glory of God and not our own. Romans 8:20–21 says:

> For the creation (nature) was subjected to
> frailty (to futility, condemned to frustration),
> not because of some intentional fault on its
> part, but by the will of Him Who so subjected
> it--[yet] with the hope That nature (creation)
> itself will be set free from its bondage to
> decay and corruption [and gain an entrance]
> into the glorious freedom of God's children.

The creation, the earth itself is crying out in earthquakes, tsunamis, floods, and droughts for those who walk in the manifested glory of the Lord to show themselves. The earth is in pain awaiting an end to the degradation happening upon it. It eagerly waits in anticipation for the true remnant of God to come forth in power and might to manifest the light of Jesus Christ.

The true light, Jesus Christ heals bodies, delivers souls, mends hearts, and regulates minds. This was His ministry while on the earth and should be the essence of ours as Christ followers. If the King of glory lives in us, why aren't we manifesting His glory? Jesus charged us with greater works than He accomplished. It is therefore our responsibility as the body of Christ to be vessels of greater works. It is our charge to show a dying world the Christ that lives within us. But in order to be vessels of the glory of God, we must first die to the flesh and be broken. It is only then that He can illuminate through us. Habakkuk 2:14 says:

> But [the time is coming when] the earth shall
> be filled with the knowledge of the glory of
> the Lord as the waters cover the sea.

In a dream, as I floated in the heavens among the stars, I saw the whole earth as a flood of water rushed upon it. Out of nowhere, a man appeared at the end of the earth and began to swim. I watched as he swam effortlessly in the mass of water that should have drowned him. Habakkuk 2:14 refers to the universal spreading of the truth, the Word of God, across the globe. God is about to release demonstrations of His glory in the earth realm like never before. He will flow through those yielded and submitted to Him, but we must be willing to pay the cost.

SEEKING THE FACE OF GOD

> And all of us, as with unveiled face, [because we] continued to behold [in the Word of God] as in a mirror the glory of the Lord, are constantly being transfigured into His very own image in ever increasing splendor and from one degree of glory to another; [for this comes] from the Lord [Who is] the Spirit.
>
> —2 CORINTHIANS 3:18

In a vision, I saw the Lord who was illuminated in brilliant colors and bright light. He held out a staff before me. As I reached out to touch it, He pulled me through Himself. After coming out of Him, I was illuminated and brilliant just as He was.

Even though Adam and Eve forfeited the mantle of glory bestowed upon them by God, Jesus has paved the way so that we can still carry the weight of glory upon our lives. Spending time in the face of God transforms us into His image. We become more like Him, going from one degree of glory to the next, in hopes that we will become temples of truth and vessels suitable to go into the world and make more disciples. We must come to a place where we desire God's face and not only His hand. Exodus 33:18–19 says:

217

> And Moses said, I beseech You, show me
> Your glory. And God said, I will make all My
> goodness pass before you, and I will proclaim
> My name, the LORD, before you; for I will be
> gracious to whom I will be gracious, and will
> show mercy and loving-kindness on whom I
> will show mercy and loving-kindness.

Moses was passionate about seeing the face of God. He had already seen God perform great miracles, so he was not asking for a display of power. He had already seen God provide, so he was not requesting provision. He wanted to see God's glory, to know Him intimately. Many have become acquainted with the power of God, but not His presence when it is from His presence that we receive power. This is why ministers living in known sin still operate in the power of God to some degree. They are living on the residue from when they were once in the presence of the Lord. But the day is approaching when that residue will wear off and if we are not seeking the face of God, we will be stripped naked and become useless in His kingdom. Exodus 33:20–23 continues:

> But, He said, You can not see My face, for no
> man shall see Me and live. And the Lord said,
> Behold, there is a place beside Me, and you
> shall stand upon the rock, And while My glory
> passes by, I will put you in a cleft of the rock
> and cover you with My hand until I have
> passed by. Then I will take away My hand and
> you shall see My back; but My face shall not
> be seen.

Many believe that God is speaking of His physical face; however, the *kabod* does not deal with physical attributes. The *kabod* encompasses the perfect beauty of God's character, His goodness, His attributes, and everything that makes Him God. The glory of God, gives insight to who He is. It allows us to gaze into His beauty, brilliance, splendor, and radiance. When God told Moses that he could not show His face, He was saying, paraphrasing, "I cannot reveal to you all of My goodness because you cannot handle it in your sinful state."

ENCOUNTERING GOD'S GLORY

The topic of the "glory of God" is as popular as the anointing among most Christians. Numerous songs and sermons are eloquently composed requesting more and more of it. Yet, many have no idea what it is they are requesting. The glory of God does not come to make us feel good, it comes to change us. Many times in the Word we see that those who encountered the glory of God were terrified or even fell as dead. It wasn't because they had seen something so horrific, quite on the contrary, it was because they saw Someone so beautiful, holy, and perfect that their unclean flesh could not stand it. Compared with the perfection of God, they finally realized how imperfect they were. Suddenly their priestly garments were seen more as the filthy rags they were because of the self-revelation of their filth. Isaiah 6:1–5 says:

> In the year that King Uzziah died, [in a vision] I saw the Lord sitting upon a throne, high and lifted up, and the skirts of His train filled the [most holy part of the] temple. Above Him stood the seraphim; each had six wings: with two [each] covered his [own] face, and with two [each] covered his feet, and with two [each] flew. And one cried to another and

> said, Holy, holy, holy is the Lord of hosts; the
> whole earth is full of His glory! And the
> foundations of the thresholds shook at the
> voice of him who cried, and the house was
> filled with smoke. Then said I, Woe is me! For
> I am undone and ruined, because I am a man
> of unclean lips, and I dwell in the midst of a
> people of unclean lips; for my eyes have seen
> the King, the Lord of hosts!

Initially, we find Isaiah preoccupied with the sins of everyone else, but when the glory of the Lord manifested he was suddenly aware that *he* was an undone, sinful, ruined, man of unclean lips. *Undone* in the Hebrew is *damah*, which means "utterly reduced." Isaiah was reduced to who he truly was in the presence of Jehovah.

Man was born in sin and shaped in iniquity, so when the glory of God is present, it utterly reduces us and reveals exactly how vile we are in comparison to an almighty, holy, and beautiful God. Second Chronicles 5:11–14 says:

> And when the priests had come out of the
> Holy Place—for all the priests present had
> sanctified themselves, separating themselves
> from everything that defiles, without regard to
> their divisions; And all the Levites who were
> singers--all of those of Asaph, Heman, and
> Jeduthun, with their sons and kinsmen,
> arrayed in fine linen, having cymbals, harps,
> and lyres--stood at the east end of the altar,
> and with them 120 priests blowing trumpets;
> And when the trumpeters and singers were
> joined in unison, making one sound to be
> heard in praising and thanking the Lord, and
> when they lifted up their voice with the
> trumpets and cymbals and other instruments
> for song and praised the Lord, saying, For He
> is good, for His mercy and loving-kindness

> endure forever, then the house of the Lord
> was filled with a cloud, So that the priests
> could not stand to minister because of the
> cloud, for the glory of the Lord filled the
> house of God.

When the glory of God enters the building, rank and position no longer takes precedence. The ushers, greeters, clergy men, musicians, psalmists, prophets, priests, doctors, lawyers, secretaries, and deacons all get a preview of who they are in light of who He is. When the glory of God manifests, all of our works, songs, sermons, and duties cease because the King of Glory has entered the building.

This leads me to believe that many are not experiencing this glory, not even on Sunday mornings where most claim to. If His glory truly came down, we would not be able to perform because we would be too amazed by His goodness and His perfection. It is when we are more concerned about removing the hidden sin from our lives and less about a program that we have truly experienced the glory of God. In the natural realm, when a king enters the building a reverent hush stills the room, often many drop to their knees, bowing their heads in submission as he passes by. How much more reverent should we be when the King of Kings enters the building. Sadly, there is a notable absence of reverence for God in the world and even in the body of Christ.

God commanded Ezekiel to go to a *plain* in order to meet with Him. (See Ezekiel 3:22-23.) A plain is a "flat or lowland." So God ordered Ezekiel to go to a low place—not a mountain top—to experience His glory. But like nimrods, many stand upon their high places, attempting to take God's glory when we belong on our faces reverently before Him.

SUFFERING FOR THE GLORY

> But insofar as you are sharing Christ's sufferings, rejoice, so that when His glory [full of radiance and splendor] is revealed, you may also rejoice with triumph [exultantly]. If you are censured and suffer abuse [because you bear] the name of Christ, blessed [are you--happy, fortunate, to be envied, with life-joy, and satisfaction in God's favor and salvation, regardless of your outward condition], because the Spirit of glory, the Spirit of God, is resting upon you. On their part He is blasphemed, but on your part He is glorified.
>
> —1 PETER 4:13–14

While it is true that God wraps Himself in light, the glory of God is also manifested as darkness, thundering, and lightning. Exodus 20:18-21 says:

> Now all the people perceived the thunderings and the lightnings and the noise of the trumpet and the smoking mountain, and as [they] looked they trembled with fear *and* fell back and stood afar off And they said to Moses, You speak to us and we will listen, but let not God speak to us, lest we die. And Moses said to the people, Fear not; for God has come to prove you, so that the [reverential] fear of Him may be before you, that you may not sin. And the people stood afar off, but Moses drew near to the thick darkness where God was.

God is not, in any way, associated with darkness. If we view Him negatively, then it is based upon our own flawed perception of who He is. Inside of the darkness, thundering, and lightning of His glory, is His perfect light of love beaming through. The children of Israel became frightened of God's manifested presence, because they did not know Him and could not discern His voice. Yet, Moses, who had an experience with God, had no fear of His voice.(See Exodus 3:1-4.) When the enemy is allowed to cloak our understanding and we open ourselves up to him, the voice of God is seen as frightening because we don't know the heart of God.

With that said, nowadays many question the hand of God upon their lives, yet want to be used mightily of Him. Like Job, they feel they are too spiritual to be tested. Based upon our perception of spiritual matters and the way God operates, Gods' judgment can be viewed as negatively (darkness) or positively (light). Getting to the glory of God will cause us to go through dark times and onslaught from the enemy.

The Spirit of Glory is the Spirit of the Lord; He is the King of Glory and when we suffer for Christ, the Spirit of Glory rests upon us giving us the capability to withstand difficulty. God's presence gives us endurance beyond the physical dimension and the permission to step over into the supernatural. We pull from the spiritual realm the strength and resources needed to survive in the natural. Second Corinthians 12:7, 9-10 says:

> And to keep me from being puffed up and too much elated by the exceeding greatness (preeminence) of these revelations, there was given me a thorn (a splinter) in the flesh, a messenger of Satan, to rack and buffet and harass me, to keep me from being excessively exalted. [Job. 2:6.]....Therefore, I will all the more gladly glory in my weaknesses and infirmities, that the strength and power of Christ (the Messiah) may rest (yes, may pitch a tent over and dwell) upon me! So for the sake of Christ, I am well pleased and take pleasure

> in infirmities, insults, hardships, persecutions, perplexities and distresses; for when I am weak [in human strength], then am I [truly] strong (able, powerful in divine strength).

Apostle Paul had a great call upon his life; he was called to open the eyes of those blinded by sin so that they may turn from darkness to light and from the power of Satan to God. (See Acts 26:18.) The Lord endowed him with what was needed to turn hearts away from darkness. But in order to keep the apostle Paul from becoming lifted up in pride, the Lord also allowed Satan to send a specific trial to buffet him. However, the trial had greater purpose. God used Paul in a greater works capacity and the trial is what caused the Spirit of Glory to rest upon him. Second Corinthians 4:15–17 says:

> For all things *are* for your sakes, that grace, having spread through the many, may cause thanksgiving to abound to the glory of God. Therefore we do not lose heart. Even though our outward *man* is perishing, yet the inward man is being renewed day by day. For our light affliction, which is but for a moment, is working for us a far more exceeding *and* eternal weight of glory…
>
> —NKJV

Where are the saints who are willing to endure for the sake of the gospel? Where are those who are willing to be struck down so that the multitudes will be lifted up? Where are the ministers of God who are willing to be mocked for the sake of the truth being told? Second Corinthians 11:23–28 reads:

> Are they ministers of Christ?—I speak as a fool—I *am* more: in labors more abundant, in stripes above measure, in prisons more

> frequently, in deaths often. From the Jews five times I received forty *stripes* minus one. Three times I was beaten with rods; once I was stoned; three times I was shipwrecked; a night and a day I have been in the deep; *in* journeys often, *in* perils of waters, *in* perils of robbers, *in* perils of *my own* countrymen, *in* perils of the Gentiles, *in* perils in the city, *in* perils in the wilderness, *in* perils in the sea, *in* perils among false brethren; in weariness and toil, in sleeplessness often, in hunger and thirst, in fastings often, in cold and nakedness— besides the other things, what comes upon me daily: my deep concern for all the churches.

> —NKJV

Apostle Paul endured knowing that he would carry the glory of God. It will take endurance to stand in battle for the persecution of the saints that lies ahead. We are in a war, and only those with the Spirit of Glory upon them will stand. Only those who are proclaiming and holding fast to the truth of God in love will last. Romans 8:17–19 says:

> And if we are [His] children, then we are [His] heirs also: heirs of God and fellow heirs with Christ [sharing His inheritance with Him]; only we must share His suffering if we are to share His glory. [But what of that?] For I consider that the sufferings of this present time (this present life) are not worth being compared with the glory that is about to be revealed to us and in us and for us and conferred on us! For [even the whole] creation (all nature) waits expectantly and longs earnestly for God's sons to be made known [waits for the revealing, the disclosing of their sonship].

The world hated Jesus, the world wanted Him dead, the world mocked Him, the world whipped

Him all night long, the world placed Him upon the cross, but it was the will of God that allowed it. The passion of the Christ should be our passion. We must reevaluate our purpose behind ministry. I hear many complain saying that they are not passionate about specific areas of ministry which is considered to be beneath them. They then reach for positions of authority and spheres of influence God has not called them to. Hebrews 12:1–2 says:

> Therefore then, since we are surrounded by so great a cloud of witnesses [who have borne testimony to the Truth], let us strip off and throw aside every encumbrance (unnecessary weight) and that sin which so readily (deftly and cleverly) clings to and entangles us, and let us run with patient endurance and steady and active persistence the appointed course of the race that is set before us, Looking away [from all that will distract] to Jesus, Who is the Leader and the Source of our faith [giving the first incentive for our belief] and is also its Finisher [bringing it to maturity and perfection]. He, for the joy [of obtaining the prize] that was set before Him, endured the cross, despising and ignoring the shame, and is now seated at the right hand of the throne of God.

Jesus had the passion to serve God in whatever capacity that was required of Him. As Christians, passion is not a desire that is self-induced from our inner being, but it is initiated by God when He gives us the desire to witness His will being done in the earth as it is in heaven. The Hebrew word for passion is *pascho* which means "to suffer." Jesus died in a way that was both painful and humiliating, but the passion for the glory of God being manifested in the earth superseded His temporal discomforts. Remember He said in the Garden, "Father, if You are willing, remove this cup from Me," but in the same breath He said, "Yet not My will, but [always] Yours be done." (See Luke 22:42.)

Let this same mind be in us! We need not develop burning passion for the task at hand. We only need a burning passion for the Task-giver, Jesus Christ. After which, everything else will fall into place. He willingly gave His life for the glory that awaited Him. He conquered death, hell, and the grave—and He lives! He lives on the inside of us! Greater is He that is in us than he that's in the world (1 John 4:4). And while great persecution comes to those who are truly called of God in these final days, I hear the Lord saying:

> Arise [from the depression and prostration in which circumstances have kept you--rise to a new life]! Shine (be radiant with the glory of the Lord), for your light has come, and the glory of the Lord has risen upon you! For behold, darkness shall cover the earth, and dense darkness [all] peoples, but the Lord shall arise upon you [O Jerusalem], and His glory shall be seen on you. And nations shall come to your light, and kings to the brightness of your rising.
>
> —ISAIAH 60:1–3

13

THE BRIDE *of* CHRIST

Then I saw a new sky (heaven) and a new
earth, for the former sky and the former earth
had passed away (vanished), and there no
longer existed any sea. And I saw the holy
city, the new Jerusalem, descending out of
heaven from God, all arrayed like a bride
beautified and adorned for her husband; Then
I heard a mighty voice from the throne and I
perceived its distinct words, saying, See! The
abode of God is with men, and He will live
(encamp, tent) among them; and they shall be
His people, and God shall personally be with
them and be their God.

—REVELATION 21:1–3

ADORNED IN A gown of brilliant white, she
glides down the aisle to meet the one she's
destined to spend the rest of her life with.
Her hair is perfectly coiffed with not a strand out of
place. Diamonds cascade about her neck, across her
wrist, and upon her earlobes. Although hidden, her
shoes are equally immaculate. She is seen by
onlookers as spotless, without blemish or flaw.   The

spotlight is upon her, she is the centerpiece of the evening. Overwhelmed by her great beauty, the bridegroom eagerly watches as his bride approaches the altar. He has been dreaming of this day and cannot wait to make her his wife. He loves her with all that is within him.

There is nothing more beautiful than the vision of a bride on her wedding day. However, much preparation goes into the planning of a wedding to ensure that everything is smooth from start to finish. In fact, the bride's attire, hairstyle, and accessories are often chosen months, sometimes years in advance. Although no one is perfect, perfection is what she strives for on that special day. Revelation 19:7, 9 says:

> Let us rejoice and shout for joy [exulting and triumphant]! Let us celebrate and ascribe to Him glory and honor, for the marriage of the Lamb [at last] has come, and His bride has prepared herself….Then [the angel] said to me, Write this down: Blessed (happy, to be envied) are those who are summoned (invited, called) to the marriage supper of the Lamb. And he said to me [further], these are the true words (the genuine and exact declarations) of God.

As a bride prepares herself in the natural, so must we as the church prepare ourselves to become the beautiful, radiant bride spoken of in the Word of God. Jesus loves us so very much and He waits in anticipation for the day that He can come and take His beautiful bride home. In these last days, preparation must become priority.

> Then the kingdom of heaven shall be likened to ten virgins who took their lamps and went to meet the bridegroom….But while they were going away to buy, the bridegroom

came, and those who were prepared went in with him to the marriage feast; and the door was shut. Later the other virgins also came and said, Lord, Lord, open [the door] to us! But He replied, I solemnly declare to you, I do not know you [I am not acquainted with you]. Watch therefore [give strict attention and be cautious and active], for you know neither the day nor the hour when the Son of Man will come.

—MATTHEW 25:1, 10-13

FOUR TYPES OF THE OLD TESTAMENT BRIDE

There are four types of the bride in the Old Testament. I believe they contain insight on how we as the church must be prepared to become the beautiful bride of Christ.

EVE, A BRIDE OF INTIMACY

For I am zealous for you with a godly eagerness and a divine jealousy, for I have betrothed you to one Husband, to present you as a chaste virgin to Christ But [now] I am fearful, lest that even as the serpent beguiled Eve by his cunning, so your minds may be corrupted and seduced from wholehearted and sincere and pure devotion to Christ.

—2 CORINTHIANS 11:2–3

Eve, the very first bride of the Old Testament and of the world, was created specifically for Adam because God said, "It is not good for man to be alone." (See Genesis 2:18.) She was to be Adam's equal, both a partner and a helpmate. Eve was a

231

vision of loveliness to Adam and to God. Genesis 2:25 says, "And the man and his wife were both naked and were not embarrassed or ashamed in each other's presence." It was not until after the Fall that they became ashamed and began to hide themselves from one another and from God.

In order to be the beautiful bride of Christ, the church must become naked before God. Nakedness speaks of living a life with an open heart towards Him. Like Adam and Eve, often as believers we attempt to hide ourselves, which is futile because not a creature exists that is concealed from God's sight, but rather everything is open and exposed to Him. (See Hebrews 4:13.) We must realize that separation from God leads to death and that it is when we are intimate with Him that He reveals to us who we are in Him.

REBEKAH, A BRIDE OF OBEDIENCE

> And Abraham said to the eldest servant of his house [Eliezer of Damascus], who ruled over all that he had, I beg of you, put your hand under my thigh; And you shall swear by the Lord, the God of heaven and earth, that you will not take a wife for my son from the daughters of the Canaanites, among whom I have settled, But you shall go to my country and to my relatives and take a wife for my son Isaac.
>
> —GENESIS 24:2–4

Abraham gave his servant Eliezer the important task of finding a suitable bride for Isaac. Not just any woman would do. Eliezer was given specific instructions because Abraham wanted to ensure the appropriate woman was chosen to be the bride of his beloved son. Realizing the importance of the task Eliezer reacted appropriately, he sought God. Genesis 24:15–18, 21 says:

> Before he had finished speaking, behold, out came Rebekah, who was the daughter of Bethuel son of Milcah, who was the wife of Nahor the brother of Abraham, with her water jar on her shoulder. And the girl was very beautiful and attractive, chaste and modest, and unmarried. And she went down to the well, filled her water jar, and came up. And the servant ran to meet her, and said, I pray you, let me drink a little water from your water jar. And she said, Drink, my lord; and she quickly let down her jar onto her hand and gave him a drink....The man stood gazing at her in silence, waiting to know if the Lord had made his trip prosperous.

After meeting Rebekah at the well, Eliezer knew immediately she was indeed the bride whom he was searching for because of her obedient spirit. Unbeknownst to her, she would become a part of something far greater than she knew because of her willingness to forfeit her plans and assist a stranger in need. She had no outside knowledge of whom it was she was aiding, but her servant's heart motivated her to serve. As the church we must mimic Rebekah and yield obedient spirits to the Lord. Genesis 24:55–58 continues:

> But [Rebekah's] brother and mother said, Let the girl stay with us a few days--at least ten; then she may go. But [the servant] said to them, Do not hinder and delay me, seeing that the Lord has caused me to go prosperously on my way. Send me away, that I may go to my master. And they said, We will call the girl and ask her [what is] her desire. So they called

233

> Rebekah and said to her, Will you go with this
> man? And she said, I will go.

Without hesitation or reservation Rebekah abandoned her own family to wed Isaac. She was willing to let go of the familiar to marry destiny. "For this reason a man shall leave his father and his mother and shall be joined to his wife, and the two shall become one flesh. This mystery is very great, but I speak concerning [the relation of] Christ and the church" (Eph. 5:31).

The Father wants the best for His Son. In this hour, He is searching for those who are willing to abandon all for Him. God is looking for a bride marked by obedience and a willingness to let go of the temporal for something greater, the eternal. He needs hearts that are truly devoted to and in love with Him. To obey the Lord and His commandments is to love Him. (See John 14:15.) This is important, because in the world in which we live, many equate loving God with Sunday morning emotionalism. We cannot love God with our emotions; we prove our love for God through obedience to His instructions. Tear filled eyes and uplifted hands should be manifestations of the love and reverence we already have for the Lord inside of our hearts. "These people draw near Me with their mouths and honor Me with their lips, but their hearts hold off and are far away from Me" (Matthew 15:8). God is not concerned with mere "lip service"; He wants acts of obedience from a right heart. (See Isaiah 29:13.) First Peter 3:1–2 says:

> In like manner, you married women, be
> submissive to your own husbands
> [subordinate yourselves as being secondary to

and dependent on them, and adapt yourselves to them], so that even if any do not obey the Word [of God], they may be won over not by discussion but by the [godly] lives of their wives, When they observe the pure and modest way in which you conduct yourselves, together with your reverence [for your husband; you are to feel for him all that reverence includes: to respect, defer to, revere him--to honor, esteem, appreciate, prize, and, in the human sense, to adore him, that is, to admire, praise, be devoted to, deeply love, and enjoy your husband].

As a wife submits to her husband who is the head of the household, so must we be willing to submit in obedience to the Lord who is the head of our lives.

RUTH, A BRIDE OF HUMILITY

And Ruth said, Urge me not to leave you or to turn back from following you; for where you go I will go, and where you lodge I will lodge. Your people shall be my people and your God my God.

—RUTH 1:16

When given the choice of returning to Moab or following Naomi to a strange country, Ruth humbled herself enough to leave behind a life where she was probably considered a pagan priestess. In exchange for her position as priestess, she chose to become a servant. She left her foreign gods behind to follow after a God whom she did not know. Recently losing her husband, she was virtually penniless, yet Ruth clung to Naomi, obeying her instructions. Because of her humility, the favor of God found her while she was in the field scavenging for leftovers.

As believers, we too must exemplify humility; in fact, we should be the examples of humility for the world to follow. Many feel as though certain tasks and responsibilities are beneath them. But with humility comes surrender to the Lord and an availability to do whatever He commands.

Ruth 3:14 says that Ruth lay at the feet of Boaz all night long. Following her example, we must be willing to lie on our faces before God surrendering our will for His will, our way for His way, and our path for His path. We must get low in order to be elevated the correct way.

> When you are invited by anyone to a marriage feast, do not recline on the chief seat [in the place of honor], lest a more distinguished person than you has been invited by him, And he who invited both of you will come to you and say, Let this man have the place [you have taken]. Then, with humiliation *and* a guilty sense of impropriety, you will begin to take the lowest place. But when you are invited, go and recline in the lowest place, so that when your host comes in, he may say to you, Friend, go up higher! Then you will be honored in the presence of all who sit [at table] with you. For everyone who exalts himself will be humbled (ranked below others who are honored or rewarded), and he who humbles himself (keeps a modest opinion of himself and behaves accordingly) will be exalted (elevated in rank).
>
> —LUKE 14:8-11

When Jesus comes back, He is looking for a bride that is pure and exemplifies holiness and humility.

ESTHER, A BRIDE OF PURIFICATION

> Now when the turn of each maiden came to go in to King Ahasuerus, after the regulations for the women had been carried out for twelve months--since this was the regular period for their beauty treatments, six months with oil of myrrh and six months with sweet spices and perfumes and the things for the purifying of the women.
>
> —ESTHER 2:12

As discussed previously, Persian kings took great steps to ensure his potential wife was beautiful. Esther was no different. She went through six months of oil of myrrh and six months of spices used for the purpose of purification before she was presented to King Ahasuerus. The process is symbolic of how we as the church must be prepared spiritually. First Peter 3:3–4 says:

> Let not yours be the [merely] external adorning with [elaborate] interweaving and knotting of the hair, the wearing of jewelry, or changes of clothes; But let it be the inward adorning and beauty of the hidden person of the heart, with the incorruptible and unfading charm of a gentle and peaceful spirit, which [is not anxious or wrought up, but] is very precious in the sight of God.

Man looks on the outward appearance but God looks at the heart (1 Sam. 16:7). In the eyes of the Lord, the beautiful ones are those willing to be purified by Him. Those who have clean hands and pure hearts will see Him.

> Come close to God and He will come close to you. [Recognize that you are] sinners, get your soiled hands clean; [realize that you have been disloyal] wavering individuals with divided

237

interests, and purify your hearts [of your spiritual adultery]. [As you draw near to God] be deeply penitent and grieve, even weep [over your disloyalty]. Let your laughter be turned to grief and your mirth to dejection and heartfelt shame [for your sins].

—JAMES 4:8–9

Purification is defined as "to rid of impurities; foreign or objectionable elements and to sanctify." It involves bringing the filthy and disgusting things within the body or system to the surface for the betterment and improvement of the body or the system. Purification is not a pretty sight because during this process, the hideous, unappealing aspects of who we are, is purged to the forefront; the things hidden beneath the surface are revealed. Esther was willing to sacrifice her beauty for temporary ugliness in order to be purified for an even greater beauty to manifest. For us, this means crucifying the flesh. In doing so, all of the things that object to the will of God is brought to the surface so that we may be clean and pure. As the body of Christ, our purifying mechanism is the Word of God. We must allow the Truth to put the works of the flesh to death so that we will have beautiful hearts worthy to be in the presence of the King. "So that He might sanctify her, having cleansed her by the washing of water with the Word, That He might present the church to Himself in glorious splendor, without spot or wrinkle or any such things [that she might be holy and faultless]" (Eph. 5:26–27).

Queen Esther was known for her ability to remain strong in the midst of harsh circumstances. But before she accomplished all of those amazing feats, before she was able to hear a word from God to go

238

on a fast, and before she received the instructions that saved her people, she was first purified.

THE COUNTERFEIT BRIDE

As discussed earlier, for every move of God, Satan counterfeits. A "counterfeit" is defined as "a forge made in imitation of something genuine with the intent to deceive or defraud; forged lacking in reality or substance or genuineness."In this hour, Satan is equipping his counterfeit bride as direct opposition to true bride. Created with the intent to defraud, this counterfeit deceives the multitudes. However, when looking in depth one can readily distinguish between the true and the false because the false lacks genuineness and it lacks substance. This counterfeit looks like the real thing but when walking the walk, they fall terribly short. Upon inspection, no fruit is found. Revelation 17:1–3 reads:

> One of the seven angels who had the seven bowls then came and spoke to me, saying, Come with me! I will show you the doom (sentence, judgment) of the great harlot (idolatress) who is seated on many waters, [She] with whom the rulers of the earth have joined in prostitution (idolatry) and with the wine of whose immorality (idolatry) the inhabitants of the earth have become intoxicated. And [the angel] bore me away [rapt] in the Spirit into a desert (wilderness), and I saw a woman seated on a scarlet beast that was all covered with blasphemous titles (names), and he had seven heads and ten horns.

The harlot above is comfortable with her evil harlotries, spreading them across the nations. She sits upon a throne as if she is a true queen. Grandiose in thinking, she says in her heart, "I have become as God." The spirit of harlotry is responsible for causing the earth to be filled with all manner of lewdness and abominations. Counterfeit Christians have become comfortable living unholy lifestyles and have forsaken holiness. Leviticus 10:10 says that we must distinguish between the holy and the common, between the unclean and the clean.

Many have become self-righteous thinking righteousness comes from their own works. Self-righteous individuals seek ways to make themselves appear holy. We must remember that we have been "permitted to dress in fine (radiant) linen, dazzling and white--for the fine linen is (signifies, represents) the righteousness (the upright, just, and godly living, deeds, and conduct, and right standing with God) of the saints (God's holy people)." (See Revelation 19:8.) We did not earn it; it was given to us by our Lord and Savior. Thus, our hearts and minds must be devoted to Him. Revelation 17:5–6 continues:

> And on her forehead there was inscribed a name of mystery [with a secret symbolic meaning]: Babylon the great, the mother of prostitutes (idolatresses) and of the filth and atrocities and abominations of the earth. I also saw that the woman was drunk, [drunk] with the blood of the saints (God's people) and the blood of the martyrs [who witnessed] for Jesus. And when I saw her, I was utterly amazed and wondered greatly.

The condition of the forehead was an important criterion in the diagnosis of leprosy by the priests of God. The forehead represents the heart and the mind. It was upon the forehead that David smote Goliath with the stone from his sling. A "harlot's forehead" is used in Jeremiah 3:3 to describe the shameless apostasy and faithlessness of Israel. And God also makes His prophet's forehead "hard," which represents undying loyalty to God's commands and a repulsion of the things that oppose Him. (See Ezekiel 3:9.) Furthermore, Aaron and every high priest after him were to wear the golden frontlets upon their foreheads which were engraved, "Holy to Yahweh." This was representative of their hearts and minds being devoted to God alone. In the end- times, Satan will place his mark upon foreheads, which represents complete control of the heart and mind.

> Also he compels all [alike], both small and great, both the rich and the poor, both free and slave, to be marked with an inscription [stamped] on their right hands or on their foreheads, So that no one will have power to buy or sell unless he bears the stamp (mark, inscription), [that is] the name of the beast or the number of his name. Here is [room for] discernment [a call for the wisdom of interpretation]. Let anyone who has intelligence (penetration and insight enough) calculate the number of the beast, for it is a human number [the number of a certain man]; his number is 666.
>
> —REVELATION 13:16–18

As Christians, the Lord instructs us to guard our hearts and to renew our minds. Why, because whatever is in our hearts and what we allow into our minds will be manifested in our hands and feet, that is, how we live. The counterfeit bride is being groomed and transformed in the image of her father, Satan. His focus is on making the counterfeit's adornment merely outward in order to deceive.

Counterfeits appear holy, but it's only an appearance. Truth is, their hearts have been turned by the wickedness of the world and purity is far from them. Upon their hearts and minds, they wear abominations, hate, lewdness, and all manner of perversity.

THE CHURCHES OF REVELATION

THE CHURCH OF THYATIRA

> I know your record and what you are doing, your love and faith and service and patient endurance, and that your recent works are more numerous and greater than your first ones. But I have this against you: that you tolerate the woman Jezebel, who calls herself a prophetess [claiming to be inspired], and who is teaching and leading astray my servants and beguiling them into practicing sexual vice and eating food sacrificed to idols.
>
> —REVELATION 2:19–20

While commended on several things, the church of Thyatira allowed the spirit of Jezebel to run rampant in their midst. She was allowed to roam freely and lead God's people astray. It is apparent that they did nothing to prevent or put a stop to it. We as the body of Christ must not sit idly as all manner of heresy is spewed from the pulpit. Until we acknowledge the problems in our midst and confront Jezebel head on, we cannot move into the next phase of resolution.

How does one take on the spirit of Jezebel and her legions of false prophets? With truth, through holiness and righteousness. The Enemy is only threatened by those who walk in holiness, righteous, and obedience. It is through obedience to God that we overthrow his works.

THE CHURCH OF LAODICEA

> I know your [record of] works and what you are doing; you are neither cold nor hot. Would that you were cold or hot! So, because you are lukewarm and neither cold nor hot, I will spew you out of My mouth! For you say, I am rich; I have prospered and grown wealthy, and I am in need of nothing; and you do not realize and understand that you are wretched, pitiable, poor, blind, and naked.
>
> —REVELATION 3:15–17

The church of Laodicea was known as the lukewarm church. Because they were lukewarm, they received no commendations. There is nothing about being lukewarm that appeals to anyone. For the most part, we tend to drink our beverages hot or cold. In fact, nothing repulses me more than taking a sip from an intended cup of hot coffee that has sat out and become lukewarm. It literally makes me want to vomit. Furthermore, it no longer has the ability to warm me up. Likewise, when I have a cold drink that has sat out and gotten warm, I get rid of it, because it no longer serves its purpose of refreshing me.

Why do hot and cold drinks become lukewarm? It is because they literally attempt to match their surroundings. Technically speaking, an object tends to come to equilibrium with its surroundings. The hot drink is at a higher energy level and loses heat to its surroundings until equilibrium is achieved. The cold drink is at a lower energy level and absorbs heat from its surroundings until equilibrium is achieved. In either case, the higher energy level loses heat to the

243

lower energy level until the two levels equilibrate. *Equilibrium* is defined as "a condition in which all acting influences are cancelled by others, resulting in a stable, balanced, or unchanging system."

Spiritually speaking, the "hot" represents those who are on fire for God. Yet oftentimes they sit in the surroundings of the world for so long, that their holy walk is cancelled by the unholy. They pick up a habit here and a wrong belief there, and before long they have become lukewarm—one foot inside of the church and the other in the world. This is repulsive in the eyes of God. "Do not be so deceived *and* misled! Evil companionships (communion, associations) corrupt *and* deprave good manners *and* morals *and* character" (1 Cor. 15:33).

The cold represents those who have nothing to do with God in deeds, yet they sit in the atmosphere of those who are holy. They live lifestyles opposing Him, yet they taint church services Sunday after Sunday with unrepentant hearts and vulgar intentions. Members who are aware of their alternative lifestyles never approach them with correction or warning, so these individuals remain in a holy place with unholy mind-sets. They know the truth yet blatantly disrespect God by flaunting their indiscretions in the very house of God. The fact that this individual is permitted to live in sin and sit in a holy place, cancels out the holy walk of others. Galatians 5:9 says, "A little leaven (a slight inclination to error, or a few false teachers) leavens the whole lump [it perverts the whole conception of faith or misleads the whole church]."

What has been created in both situations is an unchanging system of complacency and lukewarmness toward the things of God. But Jesus says, "Because you are lukewarm and neither cold nor hot, I will spew you out of My mouth!"

Many are seated in a gray area of deception, when the truth is, there is no such thing as *in between*. You either have the truth or a lie, serve God or Satan, will choose life or death. Time is out for compromise. We as the church must stand up in our God-given authority and begin to tear this system of lies spoken through the spirit of the great whore down.

THE CHURCH OF PERGAMOS

> I know where you live--a place where Satan sits enthroned. [Yet] you are clinging to and holding fast My name, and you did not deny My faith, even in the days of Antipas, My witness, My faithful one, who was killed (martyred) in your midst--where Satan dwells. Nevertheless, I have a few things against you: you have some people there who are clinging to the teaching of Balaam, who taught Balak to set a trap and a stumbling block before the sons of Israel, [to entice them] to eat food that had been sacrificed to idols and to practice lewdness [giving themselves up to sexual vice]. You also have some who in a similar way are clinging to the teaching of the Nicolaitans [those corrupters of the people] which thing I hate. Repent [then]! Or else I will come to you quickly and fight against them with the sword of My mouth.
>
> —REVELATION 2:13–16

We must overthrow the dark doctrine of Babylon which will ultimately attempt to cause many to fall into a false consolidated religion of compromise and contradiction. It is time to forsake the deception of the unholy mixture of godliness and religion, of humility and pride, self-denial and lust, hot and cold. As the church, we must challenge the false as Elijah did in his time. We must forsake the teachings of Baalam and remember that any alteration of the Word of God is blasphemy. The whole Truth must be taught in order for lives to be changed. The world is dying, and we will be held accountable as leaders and as the church, if we don't do everything in our ability to correct the harm. We must separate from religious compromise and hold fast to the Word of God, knowing that Jesus is the only Way.

We also must have true hearts of repentance. True repentance is not merely walking up to an altar and asking for forgiveness with our mouths. It's about having a sincere desire to live lives with our hearts turned toward God and away from the things that offends Him.

THE CHURCH OF SARDIS

> I know your record and what you are doing; you are supposed to be alive, but [in reality] you are dead. Rouse yourselves and keep awake, and strengthen and invigorate what remains and is on the point of dying; for I have not found a thing that you have done [any work of yours] meeting the requirements of My God or perfect in His sight. So call to mind the lessons you received and heard; continually lay them to heart and obey them, and repent. In case you will not rouse yourselves and keep awake and watch, I will come upon you like a thief, and you will not know or suspect at what hour I will come.

> —REVELATION 3:1b–3

Sardis is known as the dead church. In other words, this church is one that appears to be alive—

beautiful and spiritually vibrant outwardly, but on the inside are lies and corruption.

> Woe to you, scribes and Pharisees, pretenders (hypocrites)! For you are like tombs that have been whitewashed, which look beautiful on the outside but inside are full of dead men's bones and everything impure. Just so, you also outwardly seem to people to be just and upright but inside you are full of pretense and lawlessness and iniquity.
>
> —MATTHEW 23:27-28

This church professed to be spiritual but was impure and deceived. They had been in character so long that they'd forgotten God sees the heart. We must remain pure and holy and acceptable before the Lord. We must, at all counts, be truthful to ourselves and to Him. False pretences will get us nowhere but one step closer to judgment. Our responsibility as Christian apothecaries, is ensuring that we do not allow flies to seep in with forms of godliness. We must not allow wickedness to be considered the norm.

> For [although] they hold a form of piety (true religion), they deny and reject and are strangers to the power of it [their conduct belies the genuineness of their profession]. Avoid [all] such people [turn away from them.
>
> —2 TIMOTHY 3:5

THE CHURCH OF EPHESUS

> I know your industry and activities, laborious toil and trouble, and your patient endurance, and how you cannot tolerate wicked [men] and have tested and critically appraised those who call [themselves] apostles (special messengers of Christ) and yet are not, and

have found them to be impostors and liars. I know you are enduring patiently and are bearing up for My name's sake, and you have not fainted or become exhausted or grown weary. But I have this [one charge to make] against you: that you have left (abandoned) the love that you had at first [you have deserted Me, your first love]. Remember then from what heights you have fallen. Repent (change the inner man to meet God's will) and do the works you did previously [when first you knew the Lord], or else I will visit you and remove your lampstand from its place, unless you change your mind and repent. Yet you have this [in your favor and to your credit]: you hate the works of the Nicolaitans [what they are doing as corrupters of the people], which I Myself also detest.

—REVELATION 2:2–6

The church at Ephesus was commended, yet they had lost their zeal for the Lord. Often times, we find ourselves performing many tasks for God, but at the cost of love and zeal for Him. This often happens in marriage. A wife may become obsessed with the duties of housework, caring for the children, working, or performing other "wifely" duties but neglects her husband. A husband may become preoccupied with the task of being a provider but simultaneously ignores and abandons his wife. The Enemy divides and conquers; he separates and then slips in. We are not to forsake the call to true ministry. We should remember that it is based upon love for God and the love for His purpose, because those things will bring Him the glory. We cannot allow Satan to slip in and separate us from our true Love, our reason for breathing.

THE CHURCH OF PHILADELPHIA

> I know that you have but little power, and yet
> you have kept My Word and guarded My
> message and have not renounced or denied
> My name. Take note! I will make those of the
> synagogue of Satan who say they are Jews and
> are not, but lie--behold, I will make them
> come and bow down before your feet and
> learn and acknowledge that I have loved you.
>
> —REVELATION 3:8–9

We have discussed faithfulness at length in the previous chapters because it is the remedy for the acts of harlotry within the body of Christ. We as the church must remain faithful in the midst of a world where faithfulness is viewed as an option. Faithfulness is much needed, because without it we walk about aimlessly with divided affections, breaking the heart of God.

THE CHURCH OF SMYRNA

> I know your affliction and distress and
> pressing trouble and your poverty--but you
> are rich! and how you are abused and reviled
> and slandered by those who say they are Jews
> and are not, but are a synagogue of Satan.
> Fear nothing that you are about to suffer.
> [Dismiss your dread and your fears!] Behold,
> the devil is indeed about to throw some of
> you into prison, that you may be tested and
> proved and critically appraised, and for ten
> days you will have affliction. Be loyally faithful
> unto death [even if you must die for it], and I
> will give you the crown of life.
>
> —REVELATION 2:8–10

Persecution comes to those who truly serve the Lord. However, we have been equipped with everything we need to withstand the tests of time and onslaught from Satan.

COME

> How fair you are, my love [he said], how very fair! Your eyes behind your veil [remind me] of those of a dove; your hair [makes me think of the black, wavy fleece] of a flock of [the Arabian] goats which one sees trailing down Mount Gilead [beyond the Jordan on the frontiers of the desert]....O you who dwell in the gardens, your companions have been listening to your voice—now cause me to hear it.[Joyfully the radiant bride turned to him, the one altogether lovely, the chief among ten thousand to her soul, and with unconcealed eagerness to begin her life of sweet companionship with him, she answered] Make haste, my beloved, *and* come quickly, like a gazelle or a young hart [and take me to our waiting home] upon the mountains of spices!
>
> —SONG OF SOLOMON 4:1, 8:13-14

In a dream, I watched a famous woman named Jennifer whose name means "white" and "fair one." She wore a lovely white wedding gown as she stood in the midst of a magnificent and beautiful garden scene. I perceived that both a baptism and a wedding were taking place because the aisle, in which she walked, was a mass of water that came about knee length. As she waded through the water to meet her expectant groom, she looked at him with love in her eyes. Finally reaching him, she gazed into his eyes and said, "It's a beautiful time to build," as she turned to kiss him on the lips. The Hebrew word for "fair" is *yaphah*[23], which means "to make yourself beautiful." It's a beautiful time to gather souls to build upon the kingdom of God. It's a beautiful time to gather those who walk in the darkness of the world. "Do you not say, it is still four months until harvest time comes? Look! I tell you, raise your eyes and observe the fields and see how they are already white for harvesting" (John 4:35). It's a beautiful time for the world to be baptized into the body of Christ. May God's voice echo to the true bride of Christ, "You are fair My love and there is no spot in you." (See Song of Solomon 4:7.)

> The [Holy] Spirit and the bride (the church, the true Christians) say, Come! And let him who is listening say, Come! And let everyone come who is thirsty [who is painfully conscious of his need of those things by which the soul is refreshed, supported, and strengthened]; and whoever [earnestly] desires to do it, let him come, take, appropriate, and drink the water of Life without cost.
>
> —REVELATION 22:17

CONCLUSION

ALTHOUGH THERE IS an evident problem within the body of Christ and the world as a whole, all is not lost, because Jesus Christ has already overcome the world. (See John 16:33.) The passion of the Christ and His undying love, saved, delivered, and set us all free. He who knew no sin, became sin for you and I. Upon His body lied every sick, twisted, and perverse sin we would ever commit. Upon His pure and holy body lied every sickness and disease that we deserved as result of our fallen state. He bore it all!

He hung on the cross and died, yet His life was not taken, He joyfully gave it. "He, for the joy [of obtaining the prize] that was set before Him, endured the cross, despising *and* ignoring the shame, and is now seated at the right hand of the throne of God" (Heb. 12:2). On the third day, He arose with ALL power in His hands. He opened up a way for us as sinners to come to the Father.

However, we as the body of Christ have been deceived into believing that we still have a life, when in fact, we do not. When Jesus Christ took our place upon the cross, we died there along with the multitudes of our sins, transgressions, and diseases.

> For he hath made him to be sin for us, who knew no sin; that we might be made the righteousness of God in him.
>
> —2 CORINTHIANS 5:21, KJV

253

Because of Him we have the power to live righteous lives in holiness. Because He is righteous, we are now the righteous. The God that overcame the world lives on the inside of us. This is not in theory, this is fact. The almighty and powerful God literally lives on the inside of us! So how is it that we can continue playing the harlot? How can we put our hands to the very things that God abhors? If there is a pure, holy, and awesome God living inside of our hearts right now, how can we disrespect Him as though He does not exist at all? If our bodies are truly temples of the Holy Spirit, why do we continuously fall for the enemy's trickery? If we truly have the mind of God, then why don't we have His heart? His heart, an undivided heart is needed in this hour. Temptation will come, but with clean hearts devoted to God, we can resist it.

When the seductress of this world whispers into our ears attempting to seduce us away from God—the righteousness of God in us responds, "Man shall not live by bread alone but by every word that proceeds out of the mouth of God." When the Enemy comes to tempt us into committing spiritual suicide, defying all that God has instructed us to do— the holiness of God in us declares, "I will not tempt the Lord my God." When the god of this age attempts to lure us away with visions of false prosperity and wealth, if he brings us to even the highest mountain top or peak of prosperity, asking us for our souls in exchange—the righteousness of God in us will respond "I will worship the Lord God alone, it is He only that I will serve." (See Matthew 4:1-11.)

How do we overcome the stench that is circulating within the body of Christ and being implanted into the hearts of the multitudes? I do not profess to have a solution that is not already written in the Word of God. And although the points written below may seem elementary to some, it is quite evident that they have become increasingly more difficult for many to execute.

1. LOVE GOD WITH WHOLE HEARTS

First, as a church we must return to our Lord and Savior, our first Love, seeking to know Him intimately. This is so that His marvelous light will illuminate through us and to a world that is decaying and putrid. It is important to understand what truly loving God means. Across the globe as we speak, there are professing unrepentant sinners with tear-filled eyes, all claiming to "love" Jesus. Sensationalism is not what I am speaking of; I'm talking about true love.

> For the [true] love of God is this: that we do His commands [keep His ordinances and are mindful of His precepts and teaching]. And these orders of His are not irksome (burdensome, oppressive, or grievous).

> —1 JOHN 5:3

We must love God with our whole hearts through our obedience to His commands. If we truly love Him, we must turn and repent; if He truly has our hearts, we would change our wicked ways. If we honestly love the Lord, we must lay aside all of the weights and snares that so easily beset us. (See

Hebrews 12:1.) Now is not the time to be caught with divided affections and callused hearts, we must make our allegiance sure.

2. SPEAK THE TRUTH IN LOVE

The sweet gospel of Christ must be declared in all honesty and with great fervency. His passion must become our passion. The inerrant Word of God must become as fire shut up in our bones. We must forcefully oppose to darkness of falsehood, because when we taint the Word of God with our humanistic wisdom, we are responsible for spreading just as much decay as the world. The spirits of harlotry will only be overtaken by proclaiming the truth in love.

> The prophet who has a dream, let him tell his dream; but he who has My word, let him speak My word faithfully. What has straw in common with wheat [for nourishment]? says the Lord. Is not My word like fire [that consumes all that cannot endure the test]? says the Lord, and like a hammer that breaks in pieces the rock [of most stubborn resistance]?Therefore behold, I am against the [false] prophets, says the Lord, [I am even now descending upon them with punishment, these prophets] who steal My words from one another [imitating the phrases of the true prophets.
>
> —JEREMIAH 23:28-30

3. ARISE AND ENGAGE

Collectively, as the church, we must arise in the power and authority lying within us to overtake the heinous spirits attempting to overshadow the truth. It is after we have begun to love and obey God and after we have returned to our first love that we are able to effectively confront the spirits of harlotry head on. Through clean and anointed vessels of purity and holiness, we will speak to every principality, ruler, and power of the air commanding it to its rightful position which is under the footstool of Jesus Christ. Though the victory is ours, the battle rages and still we must fight.

> But thanks be to God, Who gives us the victory [making us conquerors] through our Lord Jesus Christ.
>
> —1 CORINTHIANS 15:57

Prayer

Lord according to Your Word in Galatians 5:16, may we walk in the Spirit, so that we will not fulfill the lusts of the flesh. May we walk in the fruit of the Spirit; love, joy, peace, forbearance, kindness, goodness, faithfulness, gentleness, and self-control. May we walk worthy of the high calls upon our lives. May we preach the Word of God unadulterated and uncompromisingly with passion and fervency. Lord, we realize and acknowledge the spirit of harlotry that the enemy has unleashed upon the world and the body as a whole. Yet we know that You are Lord of all, able to do exceedingly and abundantly and above all that we can ever think of. Lord we know that it shall be overtaken, not by our might or power but by Your Spirit. Because we are Your hands and feet in the earth, please mold us into vessels worthy to be used mightily in this hour. Transform us into vessels of honor, purity, deliverance, healing, and love. Create in us clean hearts, give us undivided minds, so that our affections will not be divided. Lord, may we forever be devoted to our Bridegroom, in the name of Jesus. Amen.

NOTES

INTRODUCTION

[1] James Strong's Exhaustive Concordance of the Bible (updated) n.p: Riverside World 1996, s.v. na'ap, 5003, "apostatize."

[2] Merriam-Webster Collegiate Dictionary, 11th Edition (Springfield, MA: Merriam Webster Inc., 2003), s.v. apostasy.

[3] James Strong's Exhaustive Concordance of the Bible (updated) n.p: Riverside World 1996, s.v. mashach, 4886, "anointing."

[4] Ibid., s.v. zuwr, 2114, "strange."

[5] Ibid., s.v. bosem, 1314, "sweet."

[6] Ibid., s.v. qinnamon, 7076, "cinnamon."

[7] Ibid., s.v. qiddah, 6916, "cassia."

CHAPTER 2

THE SPIRIT OF HARLOTRY

[8] International Standard Bible Encyclopedia, Harlot Orr, James, M.A., D.D. General Editor. s.v. "harlot." International Standard Bible Encyclopedia."bible-history.com - ISBE; 1915

[9] Online Article "The Human Side of Salt" http://www.academyhealthnj.com .

CHAPTER 3

THE INFLUENCE OF BABYLON

[10] Online Article "The Tower of Babel" by Lambert Dolphin; http://www.ldolphin.org/babel.html.

[11] James Strong, Strong's Exhaustive Concordance of the Bible (updated) n.p: Riverside World 1996, s.v. zaman, 2163, "imagined."

[12] Online Article, bible.org, Babylon as seen in Revelation 17-18; Study by J.Hampton Keathley, II.

CHAPTER 5

THE SPIRIT OF BELIAL

[13] The freedictionary.com online source "worthless.

CHAPTER 6

THE SPIRIT OF LUST

[14] Fausset, Andrew Robert M.A., D.D., "Definition for Branch Fausetts Bible Dictionary."

[15] James Strong, Strong's Exhaustive Concordance of the Bible (updated) n.p: Riverside World 1996, s.v. mammon, 3126, "wealth."

[16] Ibid., s.v. chayil, 2429, "strength, army, force."

[17] The American Heritage® Dictionary of the English Language, Fourth Edition copyright ©2000 by Houghton Mifflin Company. Updated in 2009.

CHAPTER 9

THE SPIRIT OF OFFENSE

[18] bid., s.v. mikshol, 4383, "stumbling block."

[19] Thayer and Smith. Greek Lexicon entry for "skandalon." "The New Testament Greek Lexicon." www.studylight.org.

CHAPTER 12

THE SPIRIT OF GLORY

[20] James Strong, Strong's Exhaustive Concordance of the Bible (updated) n.p: Riverside World 1996, s.v. arom, 6174, "partially naked."

[21] Ibid., s.v. erom, 5903, "totally naked."

[22] Ibid., s.v. kabod, 3520, "glory."

CHAPTER 13

THE BRIDE OF CHRIST

[23] Ibid., s.v. yaphah, 3302, "beautiful."

www.ingramcontent.com/pod-product-compliance
Lightning Source LLC
Chambersburg PA
CBHW071954040426
42447CB00009B/1326